Ida Raming

55 Years of Struggle for Women's Ordination in the Catholic Church

Ida Raming

55 Years of Struggle for Women's Ordination in the Catholic Church

A Pioneer looks back:
individuals – documents – events – movements

English Translation: James A. Turner

This book is printed on acid-free paper.

Bibliographic information published by the Deutsche Nationalbibliothek
The Deutsche Nationalbibliothek lists this publication in the Deutsche
Nationalbibliografie; detailed bibliographic data are available in the Internet at
http://dnb.dnb.de.

ISBN 978-3-643-91265-7 (pb)
ISBN 978-3-643-96265-2 (PDF)

A catalogue record for this book is available from the British Library.

© LIT VERLAG GmbH & Co. KG Wien,
Zweigniederlassung Zürich 2020
Flössergasse 10
CH-8001 Zürich
Tel. +41 (0) 76-632 84 35
E-Mail: zuerich@lit-verlag.ch   http://www.lit-verlag.ch
Distribution:
In the UK: Global Book Marketing, e-mail: mo@centralbooks.com
In North America: Independent Publishers Group, e-mail: orders@ipgbook.com
In Germany: LIT Verlag Fresnostr. 2, D-48159 Münster
Tel. +49 (0) 2 51-620 32 22, Fax +49 (0) 2 51-922 60 99, e-mail: vertrieb@lit-verlag.de
e-books are available at www.litwebshop.de

Inhalt

Foreword 7
Why is admission to ordination and priesthood and to all church
    ministries of fundamental importance to both women as well as
    to a reform of the Church?. 9
I   The beginnings of the Internal Church Women's Movement in
    the 19th and 20th centuries 11
II   The period of the 2nd Vatican Council (1962–1965) 13
III   After the Second Vatican Council. 47
IV   Developments under Pope Francis 73
V   Prospects 77
VI   Note with a view to current events 103
Appendix. 111

MOVEMENT FINALLY?!

Ida Raming (IR) in conversation with Michael J Rainer (MJR, Chief Editor, LIT Verlag)

Ida Raming "55 Years of Struggle for Women's Ordination in the Catholic Church" and also "Priesteramt der Frau – Geschenk Gottes für eine erneuerte Kirche" (LIT Verlag, 2002 –> 5579–1, 3rd edition expected in spring 2021)

MJR: *My dear Ms. Raming, I am very pleased that we are now presenting to interested readers an English translation of your retrospective volume"* 55 Years of Struggle for Women's Ordination... ", *which as you have noted met with a remarkable response and recognition. The reason for this is that the history of struggle for women's ordination in the Catholic Church has not been documented thus far. All the more reason, then, why we are anxiously awaiting and looking forward to publication of your work translated into English, which is being done by Dr. James Turner.*
The 3rd edition of your dissertation will also be coming out in the near future:

"Priesteramt der Frau – Geschenk Gottes für eine erneuerte Kirche"

("The Priestly Office of Women: God's Gift to a Renewed Church"). If we add the two English publications of your dissertation published in the USA (in 1976 and 2004), it would mean that this is already the 5th edition of your dissertation!

IR: I would like to thank Prof. Leonard Swidler for his tremendous efforts making publication of the first edition of the dissertation possible in the USA (1976): Both Arlene and Leonard Swidler were pioneers of women's ordination in the USA! B. Cooke and Prof. G. Macy were the driving forces behind publication of the 2nd edition in the USA in 2004. Prof. Macy had among other things carried out basic research on the history of women's ordination in the Middle Ages.

MJR: *Why did your dissertation that you worked on in the 1960s and completed in 1970 (1st print edition of the work) create such a sensation at that time?*

IR: The *Second Vatican Council* (1962–65) – a reform council – had just taken place. The question about the status of women in the church was put forward forcefully there for the first time, especially in statements submitted to the Council (by G. Heinzelmann, Iris Müller, Thea Münch and myself). The book "We

Won't Keep Silence Any Longer! Women Speak Out to Vatican Council II" (German/English, Interfeminas-Verlag Zürich 1964) chronicles the statements submitted by these women.

At that time it was still virtually impossible for a woman to find a professor willing to supervise a doctoral thesis, but Prof. Dr. Peter-Josef Kessler (who passed away in 1988) agreed to sponsor me in writing a dissertation in the 1960s on the status and role of women in the Catholic Church. That was also a very courageous step for him to take, as even professors were not able to escape the keen scrutiny of the Church's teaching authority.

It was the first dissertation on this subject in Germany. Not surprisingly, it sparked a pronounced reaction from some professors, at times an aggressive one: it was something completely new, something bewildering to them – I had literally "stirred up a wasps' nest".

MJR: *You then enumerated the key issues once again in your ensuing works:*

Ida Raming, Gleichrangig in Christus anstatt: Ausschluss von Frauen "im Namen Gottes" Zur Rezeption und Interpretation von Gal 3,27f in vatikanischen Dokumenten
Reihe: Theologische Plädoyers Bd. 1, 2006, 120 S., br., ISBN 3-8258-9706-0

and featuring the very interesting, programmatic subtitle

Ida Raming, Römisch-katholische Priesterinnen → Realität in der gegenwärtigen und zukünftigen Kirche!
Reihe: Theologische Plädoyers Bd. 6, 2013, 136 S., br., ISBN 978–3-643–12307–7

What was the response like? What came out of it? Including at the international level?

IR: In the wake of the Council, "Women in the Catholic Church" remained a stubborn issue – in other countries as well – and this has remained the case down to the present. I have been able to publish quite a bit on the topic: in addition to several books put out by LIT Verlag, my works have included, for example, articles in various magazines: "Orientierung", "Stimmen der Zeit", "Katechetische Blätter", "Publik-Forum", "Kirche IN", as well as an article entitled "Zum Priesterdekret "Presbyterorum Ordinis" (PO) in the important anthology "Aufbruch aus der Erstarrung – Konzilstexte vom Kirchenvolk neu kommenttiert", edited by G. Kraus, H.P. Hurka and E. Koller (LIT Verlag 2015).

All these books and articles are still relevant today, ultimately because the leaders of the Roman Catholic Church continue to oppress women, and refuse to institute needed reforms. This has led to a growing chorus of protest against this policy worldwide, including a host of publications...

MJR: *So you really received support from other countries?*

IR: Yes, absolutely; in the following period international organizations began to form, with forces coalescing to fight for full equality of women in the Catholic Church, for instance "St. Joan's International Alliance", "Femmes et Hommes dans L'Eglise" in France and "Women's Ordination Conference" (WOC), which is still very active today, in the USA, along with other organizations and movements...

MJR: I was fascinated how creatively you responded to these new constellations. You did not give up – you did not even let up. On the contrary, you courageously carried on in the face of considerable opposition – for example shoulder to shoulder with Iris Müller, with whom you produced a biographical work.

IR: Yes, we noticed at that time that quite a few men and women scarcely knew anything about the "historical-systematic" background underlying the status of women in the Catholic Church; so we set about publishing information on this "from below":

Iris Müller, Ida Raming: *Unser Leben im Einsatz für Menschenrechte der Frauen in der römisch-katholischen Kirche.* Lebensberichte – Hintergründe – Dokumente – Ausblick
Reihe: Theologische Orientierungen Bd. 4, 2007, 264 S., br., ISBN 978–3-8258–0186–1)

soon to be translated into English:

Ida Raming, Iris Müller *"Contra Legem" – a Matter of Conscience.*
Our Lifelong Struggle for Human Rights for Women in the Roman-Catholic Church. Autobiographies, Background Papers, Documents, Future Prospects
Reihe: Theological Orientations Bd. 15, 2010, 296 S.br., ISBN 978–3-643–10986–6

In this book we looked back on our long and intense struggle; we felt that we should pass on our experiences to posterity. The memoires of Iris Müller, the pioneer who spearheaded the movement (and a refugee from East Germany), are especially valuable in this regard.
The book also contains important documents, for instance correspondence with *J. Ratzinger*, at that time professor at the catholic-theological faculty in Münster, after a personal encounter with him, and correspondence with *K. Lehmann*, at that time assistant to K. Rahner in Münster, and later Bishop of Mainz...

MJR: *How do you see the role of* LIT *Verlag, the main publishing house for your writings? At* LIT *Verlag we have placed your works in a prominent place in our program genres of canon law, church history, and theology of gender. In addition to our interdisciplinary program, we also have feature programs in sociology, gender, HIS, religious science, etc.*

IR: I greatly appreciate the work of LIT Verlag and its chief editor Dr. Michael J. Rainer, who is a reliable, courageous editor and publisher. This is not something that one can take for granted. When I wanted to publish my dissertation (after it was completed in 1970), no Catholic publishing house was willing to do so (the content was too critical of the church for them ...). The interdenominational Böhlau Verlag (Cologne-Vienna) finally published the first edition of my dissertation in 1973.

In the ensuing period, LIT Verlag made it possible for me to publish the second edition of my dissertation in expanded form under the title: *"Priesteramt der Frau – Geschenk Gottes für eine erneuerte Kirche"* in 2002. Since then, Dr. Rainer, you in particular have always been very accommodating and cooperative when I wanted to publish additional works, and all of them are still topical today.

So I feel fortunate to have been published so consistently by LIT Verlag. As a result, my works were kept consolidated and were able to boost their impact: In your efforts as well as your actions, you displayed considerable courage, both as a publisher AND in the face of church policy, especially following our excommunication after we were ordained as priests in 2002.

Due to your far-reaching resonance as a publishing house, the impetus that we have been able to generate has spilled over into additional fields of theology in Europe and beyond. Ever since you began to consistently present my works in a prominent manner at conferences (e.g. the European Congress for Catholic Theology), my works have received uninterrupted attention. This has also impacted networks and organizations, for instance those in the USA, like "Roman Catholic Womenpriests" (RCWP), or "Wir sind Kirche" in Germany or the platform "Wir sind Kirche" in Austria, the journal "Kirche IN", or "AUFBRÜCHE – 50 Jahre Vaticanum II". The last important conference on "Women in church offices" was held in Osnabrück in December 2017 – all these streams and currents then served as input for a new movement of German bishops and German Catholics known as "Synodal Way", which began gathering force in Germany beginning in the spring of 2019 – see the well-represented Synod Forum 3: "Women in Services and Offices in the Church".

MJR: *It is also worth mentioning the aims, objectives and issues being addressed by the other forums there:*

- *Synodal Forum 1, "Power and separation of powers in the church – common participation and sharing in the mission".*
- *Synodal Forum 2 "Priestly existence today*
- *Synodal Forum 4 "Living in successful relationships – practicing love through sexuality and in partnerships"?*

And how do you see your motives with regard to the broader church public? Do you feel like you have been rightly understood in Rome – or more misunderstood?

IR: Even though there is still massive resistance against the ordination of women in the Vatican – it is impossible to justify this resistance from a theological or human rights perspective! The movement for the ordination of women has grown in strength worldwide.
So our cause and our concerns have also reached the "Synodal Way" (e.g. 3rd question of gender justice will no doubt also play a role in the other forums, for example Forums 1, 2 and 4 . . .

MJR: *Do you also feel sad in view of the many long years of struggle?*

IR: In the necessary struggle for the ordination of women and gender justice in the Catholic Church, I have succeeded in that I have been able to pursue an important *life task* worldwide. In essence, that is a gift in itself, and a boon in old age.
So I am not giving up; because I trust and believe that *"Truth will overcome – that truth will prevail in the end – and not lies!"*
I would like to thank you for your steadfast support, Mr. Rainer, and LIT Verlag. For your tireless support I thank you from the bottom of my heart and I also wish LIT Verlag every success!

MJR: *Thank you for the interview. I am sure that we will have many more telephone conversations, and not only short ones. And that is a good thing. Our discussions have often helped me to see through complex issues more clearly! At any rate: You can continue to count on me and on us!*

Foreword

The long and arduous fight for ordination of women – and the objective has yet to be reached!

For more than 50 years – to be more precise: since 1962 – women in the Roman Catholic Church have been fighting publicly to be admitted to ordained ministries (diaconate, priesthood and episcopate). But this objective has not yet been achieved! Resistance to complete equality of women, especially in the Vatican, but also outside the Vatican, is too fierce...

The majority of those women who have taken up this toilsome struggle out of inner conviction have either already passed away: *Gertrud Heinzelmann* (who died in 1999), *Iris Müller* (who died in 2011) or have grown old waiting. Aside from *Josefa Theresia Münch*, who was born in 1930, I am probably the last member of this group of pioneers from the early years of the struggle.

A few years ago, I wrote to some of the theology professors in Germany whose names I was aware of in order to convince them of the need for a history of the struggle for women's ordination in the Roman Catholic Church to be put down in a chronicle. In their responses to my entreaties, they also affirmed the need for such a project, but pointed out that by tackling such a research project, younger theologians would be running the risk of jeopardizing their theological teaching careers. Can one conjecture that, at the heart of it all, there is perhaps simply too much fear of official church repression? The negative ripple effects of Pope John Paul II's Apostolic Letter, *Ordinatio Sacerdotalis* (1994), cannot be overlooked in reactions like these, which is to say, at the end of the day responses of this sort offer a strong indication that freedom of research and teaching at university faculties of Catholic theology is truly a rare exception.

It is in view of this situation that I feel an inner calling to communicate key experiences and insights from the many years of commitment by myself and my compatriots to women's liberation, not least because of my age (I was born in 1932) and my frail physical condition.

I believe that it is high time for the history of this struggle to be documented to ensure that these tremendous lifelong commitments to attain recognition of the human dignity and human rights of women in the Roman Catholic Church is not forgotten.

Generations of women both present and future will be able to relate to the insight and experience handed down and carry on the struggle until the long-sought-

after victory has been achieved: 'freedom for the daughters of God'. The history of Protestant women in Germany, who also struggled for women's ordination for over 50 years before they finally achieved complete equality for women as ministers, has been documented, thereby holding up role models for others. Some very notable documentations/publications on this subject are worth citing here:
- A women's research project on the history of female theologians: "Darum wagt es, Schwestern..." Zur Geschichte evangelischer Theologinnen in Deutschland. Neukirchener Verlag Göttingen, 2nd edition, 1994.
- Härter, Ilse; Erhart, Hannelore (Ed.): Der Streit um die Frauenordination in der Bekennenden Kirche. Neukirchen-Vluyn 1997.
- Lexikon früher evangelischer Theologinnen. Biographische Skizzen, Neukirchen Publishing House 2005.

In the Catholic world, there is an absolute dearth of investigations of this sort.

This documentation is broken down according to periods of time that can be identified as decisive in the struggle for women's ordination. A variety of documents are available for each period of time, vividly illustrating events in the respective era. The women who formed the vanguard of the movement make up an essential part of this documentation. It is hoped that the documentation provided here will kindle the interest and encourage others, including the younger generation of theologians, to follow the path of their predecessors with compassion and acknowledgement, to stand up for complete equality for women and to recount the progress of history in the struggle for women's ordination until the objective has finally been attained!

Ida Raming, Dr. theol.,
Mai 2018

Why is admission to ordination and priesthood and to all church ministries of fundamental importance to both women as well as to a reform of the Church?

Should women, in spite of all the resistance they have been facing for so long now, and which they will probably continue to face for some time to come, stand up for a right to become members of the diaconate and presbyterate?

How great is the price to be paid for this struggle and exertion in human terms, but also in terms of individual health?

Is the effort even worth it in the first place? What possible benefits can be reaped by the individuals who make such a commitment as well as by the Church as a whole?

I believe that there are solid grounds for this labor:

- But all these gifts are the activity of one and the same spirit, distributing them to each individual at will (cf. 1 Cor 12:11): She gives to women and men charism/spiritual gifts which are to serve the building of the Church. Women (as well as men) are called upon to join the priestly vocation. (There are individual testimonies of women along these lines, and they are crying out for respect and recognition!) Women must be granted unrestricted eligibility to all ministries and offices of the Church so that the Church may reap the fruits of their vocation. The entire Christian community needs to embrace the responsibility for fostering vocations (cf. CIC c. 233 §1); it is especially diocesan bishops who are assigned to foster these vocations (cf. c. 385). When the Church officials in charge instead adopt a course of only allowing males to serve as priests, however, they are virtually dictating to God that God's spiritual power may only raise men to such vocations, thereby opposing God's free works with intolerable and onerous barriers void of any Spirit whatsoever! (What conceivable image of God can this possibly be based on?)
- By granting them access to all ecclesial ministries, women would finally be able to become fully fledged, equal members of the Church. As long as they are excluded as a result of their gender, they have yet to attain the "freedom of the children (or daughters) of God". They are held back as inferiors, condemned to atrophy in their personal development. They suffer, whether it be consciously or subconsciously. Through free access to all ministries in the Church, they would be able to free themselves from these shackles, to breathe the air of freedom and bestow their offerings without these bonds in the house of the Church. They grow inwardly, hand in hand with these tasks. (This has been demonstrated to us by the female Protestant ministers who have had equal entitlement to the office of pastor for several decades now – incidentally not without first having had to struggle for it: Their eligibility for

ordination and ministry has had a liberating effect for each and every woman in the Protestant Church, even if they do not aspire to pastoral ministry.) Women in office, who have been thusly strengthened as individuals, serve as role models for other women; they have the ability to lead other (lay) women along new paths, to show them new ways to shape their lives. They can "lift them higher". Women in the priestly ministry can support, advise and assist other women in their specific situation as women… Women in the church thus urgently need "sisters in ministry"! How long have women been lacking such role models and sisters in their development?!

- For men in the Church as well, free access for women to Church ministries holds out considerable advantages: Men have to gain women as equal partners and colleagues. So why not put aside their anti- and un-Christian claim to hegemony, their machismo, why not become more human, so that they can really follow Jesus, become more like Him, He who did not come to rule, but to serve humankind, who never staked out a claim to a privileged rank for himself based on his manhood?
- Equal partnership between women and men in the Church would bring the Church alive, make it more vibrant, enrich it (both with regard to the liturgical language as well as the image of God, whose purely masculine representation constitutes an undeniable diminishment and bias). The Church would gain credibility and perhaps become a role model for the "secular" world. For as long as women in the Church (and religions in general) are classified as subordinate, it will have a negative effect, including on secular society. The biblical message and promise: "Into Christ" is from faith and baptism … "there is neither male nor female" (Gal 3:27f). Thus, there is no primacy based on the human gender – this message could finally be realized in the structures of the Church through free access of women to ecclesiastical ministries. This would allow the Church to radiate glory both inwardly and outwardly.

I   The beginnings of the Internal Church Women's Movement in the 19th and 20th centuries:

Women have long been seeking access to the priesthood.

In the analysis of this period, we look back on the Women's Movement, which gradually gathered momentum following the turn of the century (i.e. at the beginning of the 20th century).

The moving testimony of **St. Theresa of Lisieux** (1873–1897) is well known:

"I feel a calling to the service of priesthood. O Jesus, ... with what love would I hold you in my hands! With what love would I offer you to the believers!
.... In spite of my small stature, it is my desire to bring the light to the people, just like the prophets and church teachers did before. I feel called upon to become an apostle. I want to travel throughout the world and proclaim your name." (quoted in: I. Raming, G. Jansen et al.: Zur Priesterin berufen. Gott sieht nicht auf das Geschlecht. Zeugnisse römisch-katholischer Frauen, Verlagshaus Thaur 1998, p. 18f. This book contains numerous testimonies of women, most of whom are still alive, describing their calling to the service of priesthood.)

How have Church leaders in high offices reacted to the deep inner conviction of these great saints? They have never even deigned to acknowledge them. It is profoundly disgraceful how women who feel a spiritual calling to priestly service have been ignored, disparaged and denied.

Church leaders have refused to confer their respect upon these women down to the present day!

The question of the status of women in the Catholic Church and, associated with this, the demand by women to be admitted to diaconal and priestly service – was voiced as far back as the 1920s in the context of the secular Women's Movement in Germany. After universities were opened for women to study there (in and around 1912) it was only logical to expect that protest against the subordination of women in the Church, above all against their exclusion from ordination to the diaconate and priesthood, would not be long in coming. Several books were subsequently published on the topic. Back at the time, women still lacked theological training – admission to regular theological studies for Catholic women in Germany only dates back to 1946. These early female advocates of access to the priesthood were at this point still unable to develop effective arguments when they ran up against a wall of reaction, especially from Church clerics. The dearth of training in historical-critical exegesis, which had not yet become an element of Catholic theology, had an extremely pernicious effect on both sides in the debate, but especially on the female agitators. The voice of protest that had been swelling up against the oppression of women thus soon fell silent, with the "Movement" fading into insignificance without having produced any concrete achievements. During the ensuing Nationalist Socialist era, women's studies and the Young Women's Movement became a dead letter.

Publications: a few examples

Ilse von Stach: Die Frauen von Korinth, Breslau 1929; Edith Stein: Frauenbildung und Frauenberufe, Munich 1956, 4th edition; Ms. Stein notes:

"In terms of dogma, there does not appear to me to be anything that could stand in the way of the Church carrying out such an unprecedented reform (opening the priesthood to woman, note of the author)".

E. Stein then contradicts herself by citing "tradition" and the "Mystery" as key reasons for rejecting the ordination of women:

"... Christ came to Earth as the Son of Man; thus, the first and foremost among Earthly beings, conceived most perfectly in God's own image, was a man – this would appear in my mind to indicate that He only wanted to appoint men as His official representatives on Earth" (p. 170). (source: Ida Raming: Frauenbewegung und Kirche. Bilanz eines 25jährigen Kampfes für Gleichberechtigung und Befreiung der Frau seit dem 2. Vatikanischen Konzil, Weinheim, Deutscher Studien Verlag 1991, 2nd edition, pp. 38f).

As is well known, this argumentation has yet to be overcome down to the present. On the contrary, church leaders and bishops are still resisting the ordination of women today (2018)!

II   The period of the 2nd Vatican Council (1962–1965)

Preliminary remark

Compared to this first movement for the ordination of women in the 1920s, the demand for equal rights for women in the Church forwarded at the beginning and during the Second Vatican Council is of far greater significance, above all because of the debate it ignited in the ensuing period.

Some women began publicly campaigning in Council petitions for admission of women to the diaconate and priesthood – a hitherto unheard of development.

What significance did this initiative have for the Council? Were there any repercussions of any consequence?

While the Council did not accept this demand in its subsequent decrees and announcements, some Council documents nevertheless contained impulses and proposals along the lines of a reform of the status of women in the Church. This could be witnessed, for instance, in the Pastoral Constitution "On the Church in the World of Today (*Gaudium et Spes*), which contained the following policy statement:

"Since all human beings have a spiritual soul and are created in the image of God, since they have the same nature and the same origin, since they, having been redeemed by Christ, enjoy the same divine service and destiny, the **fundamental equality of all human beings** must therefore be afforded ever greater recognition... Any form of discrimination with regard to the fundamental social and cultural rights of the individual, be it based on gender or race... must be overcome and eliminated because it is at odds with God's plan."

This statement, however, does not expressly relate to the status of women in the Church, and the few statements that do indeed address this status fail to go beyond a call for reform of women's status within the laity. Thus, it is stated in the Decree on the Lay Apostolate:

"Because today women are playing an increasingly active role in the entire life of society, it is of great importance that they also participate increasingly in the various areas of the Church's apostolate... "

On the other hand, some Council initiatives, although they were never adopted in Council decrees, called for more than 'merely' an improvement in the status of women in the laity. Statements made by Archbishop **Hallinan of Atlanta**, who among other things advocated women's admission to the diaconate as well as their active presence in theology and Church decision-making bodies in general, deserves special mention. Several of these statements make reference to the encyclical "*Pacem in terris*" issued by Pope John XXIII in 1963, in which the participation of women in public life and their emancipation from social dependence is referred to as a "sign of the times". This was the first time that the women's movement was viewed in positive terms and acknowledged by a Pope.

Between 1963, i.e. the beginning of the Council, and 1970, there were a wave of publications addressing the problem of women's status in the Church in general and women's admission to the priesthood in particular . . .

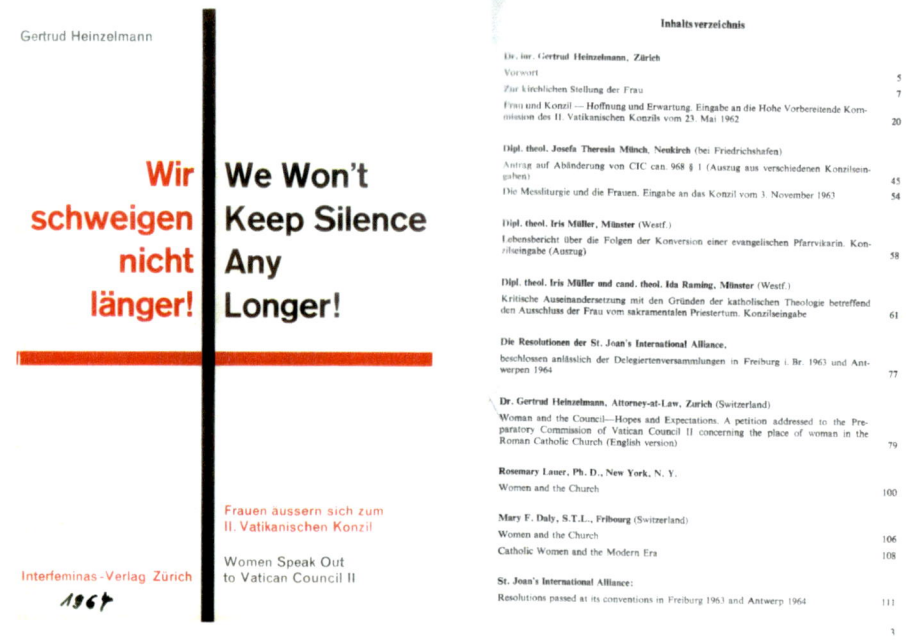

(Source: Ida Raming, Frauenbewegung und Kirche op. cit. pp. 39ff.)

PRELIMINARY REMARK 15

Vatican Council – Council Hall –
Right-hand side – Archbishop P. Hallinan of
Atlanta (USA)

Above, left to right:
J.Th.Münch, G.Heinzelmann †

Below, left to right;
I.Raming, I.Müller †

Excerpts from documents produced by the Second Vatican Council on the Role of Women in the Church

Pastoral Constitution on the Church in the World ("*Gaudium et Spes*")

No. 9 [...] Women are claiming legal and de facto equality with men as a right wherever they have yet to achieve this [...] But below the surface in all these demands is a deeper, more general aim: individuals and groups desire a fulfilled and free life worthy of human beings, in which they offer their own services to all that the world of today can offer them in such abundance.

No. 29 (inherent equality among all human beings and social justice)

Since all human beings, having a rational soul and created in the image of God, are of the same nature and the same origin, and since they are redeemed by Christ, and are afforded the same divine service and destiny, fundamental equality among all human being deserves ever greater recognition.

Certainly, not all human beings are equal in terms of physical abilities, and there are differences in spiritual and moral faculties and powers.

But any kind of both social or cultural discrimination when it comes to the fundamental rights of individuals, (whether this be) on the grounds of gender, race, color, social status, language or religion, must be overcome and eliminated, as this controverts God's message.

It must truly to be deplored that those fundamental rights of the individual are still not inviolably upheld and safeguarded everywhere; like, for example, when woman are denied the possibility of freely choosing their husband or determining their own living status, or of attaining the same education and culture as is accorded to men [...].

No. 60 [...] Women already work in almost all areas of life; but it is necessary that they be able to fully perform their roles and tasks in accordance with their own talents. It will be the task of everyone to recognise and promote each individual's own participation as well as that of women required in cultural life.

Dogmatic Constitution on the Church, "Lumen Gentium"

No. 32.2: One is therefore the chosen people of God: "One Lord, one faith, one baptism" (Ephesians 4.5); together the dignity of the members through their rebirth in Christ, together the grace of childhood, together the service to perfection, salvation, hope and undivided love. No inequality, then, in Christ and in the Church in terms of race or nation, social status or gender; "for there is neither slave nor free; there is neither male nor female. But Christ is all, and in all." (Gal 3:28 gr.; cf. Col 3:11). [...]

Just as the lay faithful, by divine condescension, have Christ as their brother who, although he is the Lord of all, nevertheless came not to be served but to be a servant (cf. Mt 20:28), so also do the lay faithful have Christ as their brothers who, placed in the holy service, with the authority of Christ, by teaching, sanctifying and leading, feed the family of God in such a way that the new commandment of love is fulfilled by all. […]

Decree on the Apostolate of the Laity "Apostolicam actuositatem"

No. 9 […] However, as women play more and more an active role in the whole life of society in our day, their wider participation in the various fields of the church's apostolate is also of great importance. […]

No. 10[…] Lay people of truly apostolic mind, like those men and women who supported Paul in the Gospel (cf. Acts 18:18,26; Rom 16:3), complement what their brethren lack and refresh the spirit of both the shepherds and the rest of the faithful (cf. 1 Cor 16:17–18).

Source: Hünermann, Peter (ed.), Herders theologischer Kommentar zum Zweiten Vatikanischen Konzil, Konstitutionen, Dekrete, Erklärungen, volume 1, Freiburg 2004 (special edition 2009)

Experiences at the 2nd Vatican Council (personal impressions and individual speeches)

11 October 1962: Question posed by theologian *Josefa Theresia Münch* at the first German-language press conference held in Rome:

"Have women also been invited to attend the Council?"

The reaction: Everything got quiet as a mouse … Embarrassment, indignation, laughter …

The chair for the press conference, Auxiliary Bishop Kampe, thereupon conjectured – partly reassuringly, partly in jest:

"There will be women, too, at the Third Vatican Council!"

(Some people at this point became aware for the first time that women had no representation at the Council whatsoever … !)

(Sources: J. Th. Münch: Zur Priesterin berufen, op cit. p. 6; G. Heinzelmann, Die geheiligte Diskriminierung: Beiträge zum kirchlichen Feminismus, Interfeminas-Verlag Bonstetten, 1986, 121)

Kard. L. Suenens (Melcheln-Brussels): Council address delivered on 23 October 1963: "At a practical level I would like to express the following desires:

So that at the Council... our faith... is illuminated in all the gifts borne by the Holy Spirit to all believers: 1. may the number and universality of the lay listeners grow; 2. may women also be invited as listeners, who – if I am not mistaken – make up half of humanity! 3. may men and women religious also be invited because they are among the people of God and have received the Holy Spirit and serve the Church... " (G. Heinzelmann, Diskriminierung p. 129; see also: ibid, Die getrennten Schwestern. Frauen nach dem Konzil, Zürich 1967, p. 9)

Archbishop G. Hakim (Greek Catholic) supported the intervention by Suenens. Intervention of 24 October 1963: He criticized the scheme for the Church because women were not mentioned in it at all, as if they did not even exist ...

Reaction to these speeches (by Cardinal Suenens and Hakim): On the one side: "tremendous applause" – on the other: conservative bishops, especially Italian ones, who disapproved of the initiative. The right-wing Italian press from 31 October 1963 mocked Suenens:

"Paladin of ecclesiastical neo-feminism... !" (Carmel McEnroy: Guests in their own House. The Women of Vatican II, New York 1996, 35, 39).

Alfredo Card. Ottaviano was one of the opponents ...

The two speeches, however, thrust the "women's question" into the public limelight at the Council, finally paving the way for a decision by Pope Paul VI to invite some women to the Council as auditors (to the 3rd session of the Council, held in September 1964 – one year later!). By the end of the Council their number had grown to 23 (religious and lay women, hand-picked!) ...

Women accounted for less than 1% of the entire assembly!

Pope Paul VI had to prevail in the face of fierce resistance! He underscored the "symbolic presence of women" at the Council!

Auditors experience considerable discrimination/disdain at the Council:

Luke Tobin (a nun from the USA) described her experiences (Carmel E. McEnroy, pp. 97 ff.).:

"Only a minority of the bishops appreciated women being present – the majority were indifferent – they avoided the women; others for their part disapproved of the presence of women...
Cardinal Felici refused to greet the women; he would not even look at them! One elderly bishop covered his eyes when he saw women going to communion in St. Peter's...
A special coffee bar was set up for women in order to avoid overly close contact with Council fathers. But the women depended on the bishops (who were their spokespersons) because they were only listeners!
"Right through the council the women had to remind bishops and theologians that they

were just ordinary human beings, and they wanted to be treated as such."
(cf. McEnroy, pp. 102–109)

"Influence" of the auditors on Council documents

Some women played a certain role on the "working commissions" (which drafted and edited the documents). Laypersons were allowed to work on the document *"Gaudium et Spes"*. All the other texts were "burdened by the sin of clericalism" (to use the words of Bishop Carter, Canada).

Prof. Bernhard Häring (bishop's secretary) supported the cause of women.

No woman was allowed to speak in the Council – although some male laymen were (they were allowed to speak 6 times!).

Lay auditor Bellosillo said that the demand for women's ordination (put forward by G. Heinzelmann and the organisation St. Joan's Alliance) was "light years" away from the Council Commission (to *"Gaudium et Spes"* – GS), where the dignity of human beings and the equality of men and women as images of God were emphasized for the first time!

Council documents only refer to women specifically in 14 places (this was also thanks to the influence exerted by female auditors).

Interventions by bishops in favor of women

- **Bishop Coderre** (Canada): denied the inferiority of women. The Church, he said, must work for the progress of women!
- **A. Frotz** (Auxiliary Bishop of Cologne): stood up for the personal dignity of women, criticizing among other things the masculinity of language used in Council texts.
- **African bishops** (for example, Malula from Leopoldville): The Church should abandon its mistrust of women and assign to them a larger share of Church tasks.
- **A Yugoslavian bishop** asserted: "Theoretical recognition of equality is useless if it is not followed up by action!"
- **Archbishop Paul Hallinan** (Atlanta, USA) contributed the most far-reaching intervention at the 4th Council session:

    "... When loudly proclaiming the complete equality of men and women, the Church must not base its stance solely on abstract theory, and must instead bear witness in a brotherly spirit... !"

It was with this in mind that he called for and recommended:
- Women be able to hold the office of lector and acolyte in Church services;

- After receiving appropriate training, women should be admitted to the diaconate;
- Women should work as theology teachers and advisors; they should participate in the revision of the CIC. – The participation of female auditors in the Council constitutes merely "the beginning of such a development…" (G. Heinzelmann, Die getrennten Schwestern. Frauen nach dem Konzil, Zürich 1967, pp. 78 f.).

This intervention by Bishop Hallinan is essentially due to the initiative of Father **Placidus Jordan** (OSB), Council theologian, advisor to the US bishops, who disseminated the book "Wir schweigen nicht länger" ("We Won't Keep Silence Any Longer! Women Speak Out to Vatican Council II"), Interfeminas-Verlag, Zürich 1964. (This book is partly in German, partly in English – note of the author.) Editor: G. Heinzelmann, at the 4th Conciliar session, among US bishops and others…

Several female theologians have published books on the subject of "Women at the Vatican Council". Above and beyond the publications already cited, the following works also merit attention:

- **Maria Prieler-Woldan**: Das Konzil und die Frauen. Pionierinnen für Geschlechtergerechtigkeit in der katholischen Kirche. Editor: The Women's Commission for the Diocese of Linz, Wagner-Verlag Linz 2013. (This book contains a detailed bibliography in the appendix).
- **Die Tür ist geöffnet**. Das Zweite Vatikanische Konzil – Leseanleitungen aus Frauenperspektive. Theologische Kommission des Katholischen Deutschen Frauenbundes e.V. (ed.), Münster 2013 (with a bibliography on pp. 140–145)
- **Marinella Perroni**, Alberto Melloni, Serena Noceti (eds.) "Tantum aurora est" Donne e Concilio Vaticano II, vol. 12, 2012, 392 pp. Series: Christianity and History, Bologna

The first critical dissertation on the topic in Germany, 'Exclusion of women from the priesthood – a tradition that is God's will or discrimination? (1970)

After passing my state examination (to obtain a teaching degree allowing me to work at secondary schools), I was able to look for a professor at the Catholic Faculty of Theology at the University of Münster to supervise my doctoral dissertation on the position and status of women in the Catholic Church, with special consideration of their exclusion from the priesthood. Something like this was exceedingly rare back at the time, in the 1960s, because even professors could jeopardize their professional careers by supervising such works critical of the existing

Church. **Prof. Dr. P. J. Kessler** (who died in 1988) supervised this extraordinary project with his expertise and knowledge, however. This deserves special mention!

It was through this scholarly work that I was able to gain deep insight into the long history of discrimination against women in the Christian tradition. To this day, the church leadership has yet to reverse ontological and moral discrimination of women, as this serves as the basis for the exclusion of women.

This research work is therefore still very topical today – including its part 2, which contains a criticism of the traditional official view of the priesthood.

- No Catholic publisher was prepared to publish my research work at that time. (For all practical purposes I was banned from professions in the Church.)
- In 1973, however, my dissertation was published by the interdenominational Böhlau-Verlag (Cologne/Vienna).
- An expanded new edition was published by LIT-Verlag in 2002.

- The work was first published in the U.S. in 1976, by Scarecrow Press, Metuchen, N.J., with a foreword by Arlene and Leonard Swidler, who provided crucial support for this first edition in the USA. 2004: Second edition of the dissertation published in the U.S. (Scarecrow Press, edited by Bernard Cooke and Gary Macy).
- For more on the content of the research by the authors and the personal consequences for Iris Müller and Ida Raming, see: **Iris Müller, Ida Raming**: Unser Leben im Einsatz für Menschenrechte der Frauen in der römisch-katholischen Kirche. Lebensberichte – Hintergründe – Dokumente – Ausblick (LIT-Verlag 2007, pp. 56–62).

The following lengthy article by Ida Raming (in: Orientierung, 65, 2001, 75–79; 86–91) addresses fundamental issues and explores the "origin and development of the Women's Ordination Movement in the Roman Catholic Church in Europe":

Women Rise Up Against Discrimination and Disfranchisement of Women in the Church
The Origin and Development of the Women's Ordination Movement in the Roman Catholic Church in Europe[*]

As a Church event of major policy significance, the Second Vatican Council (1962–65) has had a profound impact on the theological debate within the Roman Catholic Church and beyond – even now, almost 40 years since it commenced. There have been numerous theological treatises dealing with the interpretation and reception of Council decrees; scholarly works have documented and analyzed Council events in their entirety on the basis of available sources.[1]

This process is by no means complete. Obviously conditioned as well by the restorative political "climate" ascendant at present in the Church, these works concentrate especially on the ecclesiology of the Council, whereby the conception of the Church as "God's people", based on the Bible and posited by the Church constitution Lumen Gentium, is rightly attributed a programmatic, trend-setting nature[2] – with pre-eminence over any and all differentiation into various ministries, offices and estates. Only very rarely, however, does it surface that half of "God's People", namely women, were only occasionally and at a very late stage able to influence Council events in an advisory capacity (and behind the scenes), but in no instance was this influence associated with any voting rights. Moreover, women were not even present until the third session of the Council (September 1964),[3]

---

[*] (Expanded edition from the first version published in French in "Feminist Perspectives on History and Religion" [ESWTR yearbook 8/2000] Verlag Peeters, Leuven 2000, 225 – 240)

[1] Cf. the following works (this is a selection): Hermann J. Pottmeyer, et al. (ed.), Die Rezeption des Zweiten Vatikanischen Konzils, Düsseldorf 1986 (with chapters by Guiseppe Alberigo, Jean-Pierre Jossua et al.); Guiseppe Alberigo; Klaus Wittstadt (ed.), History of the Second Vatican Council (1959 – 1965) in Italian and German; vol. 1–4 of the Italian version are now available, vol. 1 – 2 of the German version, Leuven and Mainz 1997 ff.; Otto Hermann Pesch, Das Zweite Vatikanische Konzil (1962 – 1965). Vorgeschichte, Verlauf, Ergebnisse, Nachgeschichte. Würzburg 1994²; G. Vallquist, Das Zweite Vatikanische Konzil, Nuremberg 1966.

[2] For more on this cf. *inter alia*: Christian Duquoc, Das Volk Gottes als aktives Glaubenssubjekt in der Kirche, in: Concilium 21 (1985) 281 – 287; Dietrich Wiederkehr, 'Volk Gottes': theologische und Kirchliche Hausaufgaben *nach* Vaticanum II, in: Diakonia 23 (1992) 295 – 303; Herbert Vorgrimler, Die Volk-Gottes-Theologie des Zweiten Vatikanischen Konzils und die Folgen 30 Jahre "danach", in: Bibel und Liturgie 66 (1993) 67 – 72.

[3] This also applies to the phase of preparation for the Council, cf. J.A. Komonchak, Der Kampf für das Konzil (1960 – 1962), in: G. Alberigo, K. Wittstadt (eds.), Geschichte (cf. Note 1): "Of course no women, either lay or religious, were members of a commission" (201). In view of

and after this point only a small group was present as mere listeners (auditors) without any voting rights. Even less attention is paid in this context to the fact that immediately before and during the Council, it was women in Europe who took the initiative to clearly expose this harsh discrimination against the female gender and confront the purely male Church Assembly with the demand for a status and value of women in the Church in tune with the times, i.e. admission of women to the diaconate and presbyterate.

It is against this background that this pioneering work performed by women in the context of the Second Vatican Council is discussed in the following in order to keep alive the memory of a campaign that was by no means self-evident in the ecclesial milieu of that time – a campaign which has so far been ignored in historical accounts of the Council related from a male perspective.

As for the churches of other Christian denominations which already recognize the ordination of women and hence the equal rights of women, the same applies as in the case of the Roman Catholic Church: It has first of all not been males in churches who have paved the way and opened spiritual ministries to women (quite to the contrary, in many instances men have opposed it!). It has been women who put the wheels of change into motion. They have questioned their oppression in the Church and as Christians demanded full membership rights, which they are entitled to on the basis of faith and baptism. And it has been women who in line with their religious calling to serve have striven for unrestricted admission to the ministries and offices of the church.[4]

---

the status and position of women in the Roman Catholic Church, this is indeed self-evident, but who takes offence at the words "of course"? When already before the Council it was criticized that lay people were not involved in preparation of the Council (ibid. 201f with comments), this was above all with male lay persons in mind.

[4] In the following overview (which is limited in scope), I confine myself to tracing the beginnings and gradual development of the Women's Ordination Movement in the Roman Catholic Church of Europe. Broader consideration of all Christian denominations would only be feasible within the framework of a larger-scale research project. Similar developments in the "Women's Ordination Movement in other Christian churches are also described in the following literature: "*Darum wagt es, Schwestern...!" Zur Geschichte evangelischer Theologinnen in Deutschland*, edited by Frauenforschungsprojekt zur Geschichte der Theologinnen. Göttingen (Neukirchen: Neukirchener Verlag 1994); Dagmar Herbrecht, Ilse Härter, Hannelore Erhart (eds.), *Der Streit um die Frauenordination in der Bekennenden Kirche, Quellentexte zu ihrer Geschichte im Zweiten Weltkrieg*, (Neukirchen-Vluyn 1997) (Protestant). Jacqueline Field-Bibb, *Women Towards Priesthood. Ministerial Politics and Feminist Practice* (Cambridge: Cambridge University Press 1991); Susan Dowell / Jane Williams, *Bread, Wine and Women. The Ordination Debate in the Church of England*, (London: Virago Press 1994), (Methodist and Anglican). Urs von Arx, "Die Debatte über die Frauenordination in den Altkatholischen Kirchen der Utrechter Union", in: Denise Buser / Adrian Loretan (ed.), *Gleichstellung der Geschlechter. Ein Beitrag zur menschenrechtlichen und ökumenischen Diskussion*, Freiburger Veröffentlichungen zum Religionsrecht 3, (Freiburg/Schweiz Universitätsverlag 1999) 165 – 211; Angela Berlis,

So who were these women who spearheaded the Women's Ordination Movement in the Roman Catholic Church? What reactions did they encounter among men and women? Were they able to "make a difference" in the course of the Council and afterwards – for example, did they register a positive resonance or even achieve some progress? These obvious questions are addressed in the following from the perspective of a devoted witness to events at the time.

It is of course not possible to recount developments in their entirety in any detail during and after the Council. Instead, certain crucial events are highlighted. In addition, the discussion concentrates primarily on developments within Europe, more specifically in Switzerland and Germany, as the first impetus for women's ordination (and the Women's Ordination Movement) came mainly from women in these countries, afterwards spilling over into, and being strengthened by, other countries (particularly the U.S.).[5]

Pre-conciliar image of women

Roman Catholic women formulated the question of, and demand for, women's ordination for the first time[6] in official form in the early 1960s (in Council petitions),

---

Die Frauenordination – ein Testfall für Konziliarität, in: Concilium 35 (1999), 77 – 84 (Old Catholic); Elisabeth Behr-Sigel, *Le ministère de la femme dans l'Église* (Paris 1987); Thomas Hopko (ed.), *Women and the Priesthood*, (Crestwood N.Y: St. Vladimir's Seminary Press 1999), 2nd substantially modified edition (Orthodox).
See also the survey of the literature by René J.A. van Eyden in: Haye van der Meer, *Priestertum der Frau? Eine theologiegeschichtliche Untersuchung* (Freiburg: Herder-Verlag 1969) 197 – 213. Cf. furthermore the bibliography on woman and the ministry of priesthood in: Ida Raming, Gertrud Jansen, Iris Müller, Mechtilde Neuendorff (ed.), *Zur Priesterin berufen. Gott sieht nicht auf das Geschlecht. Zeugnisse römisch-katholischer Frauen,* (Thaur: Druck- und Verlagshaus Thaur 1998) 248 – 255.

[5] Cf. also Leonard and Arlene Swidler (eds.), Women Priests. A Catholic Commentary on the Vatican Declaration, New York 1977, 5. L. Swidler describes the Council submission by Gertrud Heinzelmann (1962) as the beginning of the debate over women and the priesthood; cf. also Carmel McEnroy, Guests in Their Own House. The Women of Vatican II, New York 1996, 40f, 223, 270.

[6] In the course of the secular women's movement, after the opening of university study and the political right to vote for women, the position of women in the Catholic Church and their admission to the diaconate, more rarely to the presbyterate, were already being discussed by individual women in the 1920s and early 1930s. The following authors deserve special mention here: Hildegard Borsinger, Rechtsstellung der Frau in der katholischen Kirche, Leipzig 1930 (Diss.), cf. also Edith Stein, Beruf des Mannes und der Frau nach Natur- und Gnadenordnung (1932), in: ibid.: Frauenbildung und Frauenberufe, Munich, 4th ed. 1956, pp. 169 – 171; Josephine Mayer, in: Hochland 36 (1938/39) 107, which however concentrates on the diaconate of women. Not least due to the lack of training in historical-critical exegesis (which was forbidden until 1943!) and as a result of the Second World War, these isolated voices soon fell silent. For more details on this, cf.: Ida Raming, Frauenbewegung und Kirche. Bilanz eines 25jährigen Kampfes für Gleichberechtigung und Befreiung seit dem 2. Vatikanischen Konzil. Weinheim 1991[2],

thereupon finding themselves confronted with an image of women dominated by notions of secondary status, inferiority and servitude of women. Vestiges of more than a thousand years of oppression of women in Christianity could still be perceived and felt everywhere, especially in the Catholic world, which was particularly influenced by these traditions. The demand for subordination of women to men in marriage, family and society was justified in official church statements citing biblical passages along these lines taken from the ancient "house tablets" (cf. Col 3.18 – 41; Eph 5.22 – 6.9 et al.) and propagated as "God's order": "God Himself" subordinated women to "this authority in the order of nature and grace"[7]. After the Second World War, the obligation to subordinate women in official church documents was increasingly sidestepped and avoided, but the description of the nature and tasks of women – in contrast to men – is still clearly marked by the predominance of men over women. Thus, in 1956, Pius XII declared that there was "perfect equality between the sexes in terms of fundamental personal values", but that they had "different functions" and therefore also "different rights and duties". On the basis of Gen 1.28 the woman is "not denied any human field of activity per se", this is, however, "always in subordination to the primary functions which are prescribed to her by nature itself"[8]. The "primary functions" of women are deemed to be maternity and housework; the basic types and traits of women are accordingly: wife and mother, and in the field of religion: religious order and virgin. The modern working woman in secular society, whose fields of activities are constantly expanding, is beyond the province of perception of Catholic officeholders. Such women have instead been regarded as "degenerate" because they fail to conform to their appointed purpose as women.

First Council submission for women's ordination

In was in this atmosphere, prevailing over large parts of the Roman Catholic world, that the demand for ordination of women was raised publicly and vigorously for the first time: In May 1962, in the run-up to the Second Vatican Council (1962 – 1965), Gertrud Heinzelmann (who died in September 1999), a Swiss lawyer holding a doctorate in law, sent a comprehensive submission to the Preparatory Commission. It was the "first and only Council submission put forward during the preparatory period which confronted the Church with the un-

---

38f; Friederike Kukulla, Der Streit um den Diakonat der Frau – Zur Entwicklung vor dem II. Vatikanischen Konzil, in: Peter Hünermann u.a. (ed.): Diakonat. Ein Amt für Frauen in der Kirche – Ein frauengerechtes Amt? Ostfildern 1997, 304 – 308.

[7] Pius XII: Address from 10 September 1941, in: Pius XII: Das Ideal der christlichen Ehe. Ansprachen an Braut- und Eheleute. Lucerne 1946², 197,195. For more details on this Pope's attitude towards women, cf.: Raming, Frauenbewegung (see note 6), pp. 22 – 24.

[8] Quoted in Raming, Frauenbewegung, 24.

tenable traditional status of women and the postulate of fundamental equality at all levels of Church life."[9] It was the intention of Pope John XXIII, who had convened the Council, to strive for a dialogue with the modern world to the best of the Council's ability, i.e. to strive for an 'aggiornamento'. Gertrud Heinzelmann accordingly articulated her intention in forwarding her submission as follows: "The Church, which had not even come to terms with the Enlightenment, let alone the women's movement with its cultural, legal and social context, was to receive the confrontation it was looking for."[10]

In the early 1960s, the topic of "women and the Church" was in no way virulent. This was indicated by a "survey on the Council" carried out by the magazine Wort und Wahrheit (1961): Of the 81 people who took part in the survey, only five were women. One of them (Ida Friederike Görres) opposed any attention being afforded to the women's issue in the Council, while two other women did not even mention the women's cause. Only one, Erika Weinzierl-Fischer (Vienna), "proposed a partial revision of the philosophical edifice of scholastics, stating that the position of the woman in the ecclesiastical realm was still firmly based on a derogatory appraisal of the woman contained in the summa theologica of St. Thomas"[11]. The demand for equal rights for women in the domain of the Church was completely absent. For Gertrud Heinzelmann, this was the immediate cause for action. A Catholic woman and lawyer who had already been campaigning for many years for the political right for women to vote in Switzerland, she was aware of the fateful anti-feminist influence of church norms on society as a whole. While working on her dissertation on the subject of state church law[12], she had come across misogynistic statements made by church fathers and teachers and had put together an extensive collection of texts by Thomas of Aquinas accompanied by her own critical comments, which she then used in drafting the Council submission.

Her submission contains a critical analysis of the ontic image of the woman (influenced by Aristotelian ideas) as voiced by Thomas of Aquinas, who is assigned special authority by the official church as a church teacher. Gertrud Heinzelmann derived the principal possibility and demand for ordination of women from Thomas' positive statements regarding the spiritual nature of man and the sacraments in general. She was guided by the hope that "once the ballast

---

[9] Gertrud Heinzelmann, Die geheiligte Diskriminierung. Beiträge zum kirchlichen Feminismus, Bonstetten 1986, 90.
[10] Heinzelmann, ibid., 96.
[11] Heinzelmann, ibid., 109, 112.
[12] The topic of the dissertation was: Das grundsätzliche Verhältnis von Kirche und Staat in den Konkordaten (The fundamental relationship between the Church and state in the Concordats" (issue 98 of Zürcher Beiträge zur Rechtswissenschaft), Aarau 1943.

of medieval natural doctrine regarding women has been formally cast overboard by the official Church, the path of women to the priesthood would be opened – this on the basis of Thomistic doctrine in its distilled form, the philosophia rationalis regarding human beings themselves. In the wake of the first-time publication of her submission in the bulletin of the Zurich Association for the Right of Women to Vote, Die Staatsbürgerin (July/August 1962), she was convinced "that she had achieved a leap forward that was irreversible"[13]. Even a later Council would be forced to recall that the demand for full equality for women in the Church and the ministerial priesthood had already been forwarded back at that time, at the Second Vatican Council."[14]

Thanks to the tremendous journalistic dedication of Placidus Jordan OSB, correspondent for the NC News Service at the National Bishops' Conference of the USA and Peritus of the American bishops at the Council – Gertrud Heinzelmann's Council submission was subsequently widely disseminated not only in circles of the Council Fathers, especially the US bishops, but above and beyond these circles in numerous countries as well.[15]

... the discussion begins to snowball

As was to be expected, the submission provoked violent reactions both for and against it thanks to its rapid dissemination[16]. Rude, insulting invectives, tirades of ridicule and mockery were heaped upon the author – at first mostly in a few Swiss newspapers. On the other hand, positive reactions to the Council submission showed "that the thoughts and ideas of many persons, wresting with the same problems, were moving in the same direction at the same time"[17]. So it was that initial contacts developed with German theologians. One of these, Josefa Theresia Münch, who had a Diplom degree in theology, had already directed several written (unpublished) petitions to the Vatican since 1959 calling for the amendment of Church Law (can. 968, §1 CIC/1917), which excludes women from being ordained to the priesthood[18]. In the early 1960s, female students who were enrolled at the Catholic Theological Faculty at the University of Münster at the time – first and foremost Iris Müller, somewhat later together with the author (Ida Raming) – had also critically examined the reasons for the exclusion of women from ordination and priesthood; this debate formed the basis for their subsequent submission to the Council in 1963. Eventually they learned of Gertrud Heinzelmann's submis-

---

[13] Heinzelmann, Diskriminierung (cf. Note 9) 97.
[14] Heinzelmann, ibid., 112.
[15] For more about Father Jordan and his work, cf.: Heinzelmann, ibid., 114f and following.
[16] Cf. Heinzelmann, ibid., pp. 115 – 121.
[17] Heinzelmann, ibid., p. 90.
[18] Cf. Ida Raming et al. (ed.), Priesterin (cf. note 4), pp. 53, 64f.

sion to the Council. Following this, the three aforementioned German theologians met G. Heinzelmann personally in Münster in 1963. After hearing about Heinzelmann's submission to the Council, Rosemary Lauer, Dr. phil., who was teaching philosophy at St. John's University in New York at the time, reached out seeking contact in 1963. Lauer published several articles in the widely read magazine Commonweal on the subject of 'women and the Church'. In the ensuing period, she also provided an English translation of G. Heinzelmann's submission to the American press.[19]

It was by virtue of these publications that Mary Daly first became aware of Gertrud Heinzelmann's submission. Daly studied Catholic theology at the University of Fribourg in the 1960s, where she was the first woman and American to receive a doctorate in theology in 1964. At that time, it was not yet possible for women to obtain a doctorate in Catholic theology in the U.S... Mary Daly also contacted Gertrud Heinzelmann. In a letter to the editor of *Commonweal* magazine (14 February 1964), she confessed that she felt ashamed – of herself and of all other women who "were aware of, but nevertheless remained silent about, the semi-human status of women in the Church". She foresaw a wave of books on women and the Church in the future "along the lines of a prophecy and a promise".[20]

The book *Wir schweigen nicht länger! Frauen äussern sich zum II. Vatikanischen Konzil. We Won't Keep Silence Any Longer! Women Speak Out to Vatican Council II*, published by Gertrud Heinzelmann in 1964 with parts of the book being in English and parts in German, emerged from her contact with these six women.[21] In addition to the submission by Gertrud Heinzelmann (in German and English), this work contains the Council submission of Josefa Theresia Münch as well as that of Iris Müller and the author of this book (Ida Raming) along with articles by Rosemary Lauer and Mary Daly from the period of the Council. It also contains resolutions adopted by the St. Joan of Arc's International Alliance (Alliance Internationale Jeanne d'Arc[22]), an international organization of Catholic women which was the only Catholic organization to speak out in favor of admitting women to the diaconate and presbyterate, the appointment of women to Council commissions and other reforms, including abolition of laws discriminating against women in ecclesiastical law, at its delegate meetings held in 1963 and 1964 during the Second Vatican Council.

---

[19] Heinzelmann, Diskriminierung (cf. note 9), pp. 122f.
[20] Heinzelmann, ibid., 123.
[21] Published by Interfeminas-Verlag Zürich, which had been founded by G. Heinzelmann since no Roman Catholic publishing house was willing to print it!
[22] For more about this organization, cf.: Heinzelmann, Diskriminierung (see Note 9), 216f.

For the first time, this book offers a systematic, critical analysis of the sundry biblical and dogmatic reasons cited for exclusion of women from the priesthood. By way of conclusion, the work goes on to demand full equality of women for admission to offices in the Roman Catholic Church. In addition, Ms. Heinzelmann calls for, among other things, reform of predominately masculine wordings contained in liturgical language. The public debate over the ordination and priesthood of women received considerable impetus from this publication. Numerous reviews appeared in European countries, including articles in journals supporting and opposing the demands voiced in the book.[23]

Pacem in terris: Human rights for women

Even before publication of the book, Council Pope John XXIII had furnished a strong impetus to the nascent internal Church Women's Movement through his encyclical *Pacem in terris* (1963). The central idea posited in this text[24] is that unconditional recognition of the personal dignity of every human being, which is based on the divine image of woman and man, is a prerequisite for orderly human coexistence characterized by truth, justice, peace and freedom. The nature of human beings, i.e. their human dignity, gives rise to inalienable rights and duties, irrespective of gender, race, economic or social status. For the first time in papal doctrine, women are perceived as subjects and holders of human rights, as John XXIII considered the Women's Emancipation Movement to be a "sign of the times" that had to be paid heed to. Emancipation of women was thus assessed in a positive light for the first time in the history of the Papacy: "Women, who today are becoming ever more aware of their human dignity, are not even remotely prepared to be regarded as soulless beings or mere instruments; rather, they are demanding that they be assigned rights and duties commensurate with the dignity of a human being, both in domestic life and in the state". Although no direct conclusions were drawn from this statement with regard to the status of women in the Church, ensuing statements were, however, to be applied without restriction to women – including in the domain of the Church – because human dignity is one, equally possessed by both genders and based on "equality in the one human, rational nature, which excludes gender-specific subordination of women"[25]. Recognition of this cannot and must not be restricted, for instance, to the 'secular'

---

[23] Further details can be found in Heinzelmann, ibid., 130ff with corresponding notes.
[24] Encyclical Letter Pope John XXIII from 11 April 1963: *Pacem in terris,* Katholische Nachrichtenagentur Bonn 1963, esp. pp. 5 – 15 (the following quotations are taken from this first part). The Encyclical is regarded as a Catholic charter of human rights.
[25] Helmut Hoping, Der Ausschluss von kirchlichen Weihämtern aufgrund des Geschlechts. Ein kirchlicher Modernitätskonflikt, in: D. Buser and A. Loretan (eds.), Gleichstellung (cf. Note 4), pp. 38 – 51, here: p. 38.

sphere: "Moreover, people have the inviolable right to choose the way of life that they prefer: that of founding a family in which man and woman have equal rights and duties, or that of being able to take up the priesthood or join a religious order." This is based on the principle "that every individual has the sovereign right to decide over their own life". "If, then, individuals gain an awareness of their rights, this must also give rise to an awareness of one's duties, so whoever has certain rights at the same time has the duty to claim these rights as a symbol of their dignity, but other individuals then have a duty to also recognize and respect these".

Did these words of John XXIII, together with the Council's submissions propagated by the journalistic efforts of Placidus Jordan, have any positive effect on subsequent Council events along the lines of a reform of the status of women?

Women at the Council

The Council was opened on 11 October 1962 as a purely male affair. As early as the first German-language press conference, Josefa Theresia Münch, who had a *Diplom* degree in theology, posed the legitimate, and at the same time provocative, question as to whether women had also been invited to the Council. "This prompted embarrassment, indignation and laughter. Finally, the director of the German Press Centre, Auxiliary Bishop Kampe, rejoined half consolingly, half in jest: 'Women will also be present at the III Vatican Council!'[26] "But male laymen were not present at the beginning of the Council, either, which meant that the Council Commission, which was responsible for drafting the Decree on the Lay Apostolate, paradoxically worked completely without lay participation during the first session of the Council. It was not until the second session, in September 1963, that 13 lay men were invited to take part as auditors[27]. Looking back, one of the Canadian bishops (Bishop Carter from Sault St. Marie) also expressed his regret that laypersons had been officially consulted "too little and too late", as the Canadian bishops were strong advocates of a de-clericalization of the decree on laypersons.[28]

In order to bring women as completely ignored members of the Church within the radar of the Council, a special initiative was needed: it was Belgian Cardinal

---

[26] Heinzelmann, Diskriminierung (cf. Note 9), p. 121. cf. also: Bericht von J. Th. Münch, in: I. Raming et al. (ed.), Priesterin (cf. Note 4), pp. 66f; C. McEnroy, Guests (see Note 5), p. 14 ("Th. Münch put the question to provoke thinking about it.").

[27] Rosemary Goldie, La participation des laïcs aux travaux du Conseil Vatican II, in: Revue des sciences relgieuses 62 (1988) 1, pp. 55 – 73, here: pp. 63f. A total of 29 male auditors were invited.

[28] According to Goldie, ibid. 62, note 27, they criticized indications of a sin of clericalism ('peccatum clericalismi') in the lay decree.

Leo Suenens who became (at the 2nd session, held on 22 October 1963) the first of the Council Fathers to take offence at the complete absence of women at the Council in his memorable speech on the charismatic dimension of the Church. He proposed, among other things, that the "number and universality of lay listeners be increased" and that women also be invited as auditors – adding with a certain irony: "Women, ... who if I am not mistaken, make up half of humanity".[29]

Even though "this intervention by the Belgian Cardinal was received with tremendous applause by the Council"[30] and was considered nothing short of a sensation, it did not lead to any change in course whatsoever on issues of concern to half of the Church's members, namely women.

This is shown very clearly by the feeble reaction on the part of Church leaders to this "push". Some women were admitted as auditors at the beginning of the third session of the Council (September 1964) by decision of Pope Paul VI[31]. By the end of the Council, the number of women had grown to a total of 23 (lay and religious women). Three of the auditors, including Sr. M. Luke Tobin, S.L., then President of the Conference of Superiors of Girls' Institutes in the U.S., and an Australian, Rosemary Goldie, Executive Secretary of the Standing Committee of the International Congresses for the Lay Apostolate (CO-PECIAL), were assigned to commissions working on the final version of Council documents on the Lay Apostolate (AA) and on the "Church in the Modern World" (GS)[32]. The auditors were given the right to speak in these commissions, but no voting rights,

---

[29] Yves Congar, Hans Küng and others (ed.), Konzilreden. Einsiedeln 1964, 28. P. Xavier Tilliette (in: Etudes, juin 1965, p. 824) coined in this context the expression *le sexe inexistant* for the manner in which women are dealt with in the Catholic Church – i.e. by taking no notice of women and their denial; in this connection cf. Gertrud Heinzelmann, Die getrennten Schwestern. Frauen nach dem Konzil. Zürich 1967, pp. 10f.

[30] Wolfgang Seibel, Luitpold Dorn, Tagebuch des Konzils. Die Arbeit der zweiten Session. Nuremberg – Eichstätt 1964, pp. 92f. The proposal made by Cardinal Suenens was seconded by the Greek Catholic Archbishop Hakim, but met with the strong disapproval of conservative bishops, especially Italian ones (McEnroy, [see note 5] 35, 39). In the right-wing Italian press (*Il Borghese* from 31 October 1963) there was no lack of mocking, misogynistic remarks about the initiative by Cardinal Suenens, the "Paladin of Church Neo-Feminism". Even the editor of the London *Tablet* said: "I had hoped to be appointed lay auditor of the Council soon, but now it looks as if my wife will beat me to it" (Xavier Rynne, Brief aus dem Vatikan. Die zweite Sitzungsperiode des Zweiten Konzils, Cologne – Berlin 1964, p. 145).

[31] The names and functions of the auditors are listed in Luitpold Dorn, Georg Denzler, Tagebuch des Konzils. Die Arbeit der dritten Session, Nuremberg – Eichstätt 1965, p. 431; Wolfgang Seibel, Luitpold Dorn, Georg Denzler, Tagebuch des Konzils. Vierte Session, Nuremberg – Eichstätt 1966, pp. 398f. The majority are women religious, but there are also chairpersons of Catholic women's associations. The documentary monograph by C. McEnroy (cf. Note 5) relates experiences of female auditors during the Council period.

[32] Cf. Rosemary Radford Ruether, The Place of Women in the Church, in: Adrian Hastings (Ed.), Modern Catholicism. Vatican II and after, London 1991, pp. 260 – 266, here: p. 261.

even though their own status was the very issue at stake. Although this arrangement also applied to the male lay auditors, four of them were at least allowed to deliver a prepared speech in the Council Hall. This opportunity was not granted to any woman, however. In a show of solidarity with their sisters, the auditors had demanded that at least one of the speeches should be given by a lay woman; this had even met with the support of several cardinals. Their efforts were unsuccessful, however: the demand was rejected as "premature"[33]. Thus, during the last two Council periods the few lay auditors were only able to have a very limited influence on the drafting of the said Council documents; their presence was essentially "merely of symbolic importance"[34]. Even for the laypersons who worked on the respective commissions, it was extremely difficult to make any real contribution to the final version of the decrees, as the rhythm of Council work picked up at a constant pace; above all, they were dependent on the mediation of Council Fathers or an influential peritus,[35] as women were excluded from the process of adopting the Council's binding documents right from the outset because of their inferior status in the Church; thus proposals for a reform of their situation could at most be introduced indirectly.

Statements regarding the 'women's issue' in Council documents

Despite these tight constraints, the few statements issued by the Council on the subject of women in society and the Church probably did not come about entirely without some input from the lay auditors[36]. The following statements of a programmatic, appellative nature were issued in this connection:

The Pastoral Constitution *Gaudium et Spes* (n. 29) emphasized the fundamental equality of all human beings and, based on this, the need to recognize human rights: "Since all human beings have a spiritual soul and are created in God's own image, since they are of the same nature and the same origin, since, as redeemed by Christ, they enjoy the same divine vocation and destiny, the fundamental equality of all human beings must therefore be increasingly recognized.

---

[33] Cf. Heinzelmann, Schwestern (see Note 29), p. 5; Goldie (see Note 27), p. 65, Note 34.

[34] Thus, in accordance with Paul VI's announcement on 8 September 1964 inviting women to serve as auditors (cf. McEnroy 43f), Mother Maria Brüning, Superior of the Ursulines in Dorsten and Chairwoman of the Order Superiors in Germany, who, together with Sr. Juliane, the "Poor Maid of Jesus", was appointed as the first German Council auditors. She admitted, however, that there were too few women who could make an independent contribution to the theological debate (KIPA 11 December 1964/ 674; cited by Heinzelmann, Diskriminierung (cf. Note 9), p. 159, Note 44).

[35] For more about this: Goldie (cf. note 27), p. 69.

[36] According to R. Radford Ruether (Note 32), p. 261, the presence of female auditors was an essential prerequisite for the insertion of the reference to discrimination against women and human rights for women; similar to Goldie (see Note 27), p. 72.

Certainly not all human beings are at the same level as regards their different physical abilities and their different spiritual and moral powers. But any form of discrimination involving the fundamental social and cultural rights of individuals, be it on the grounds of gender or race, color, social status, language or religion, must be overcome and eliminated, as this stands in contradiction to God's plan. It is a deplorable fact that these fundamental individual rights are still not inviolable; when a woman is denied the right to freely choose her husband and marital status, or women are shut off from achieving the same level of education and culture allowed to men." The Constitution on the Church, Lumen Gentium (no. 32, para. 2), in similar fashion emphasizes the equality and unity of all members of "God's People" – the Church: "One, then, is the chosen people of God: 'One Lord, one faith, one baptism' (Eph 4:5); together the dignity of the members from their rebirth in Christ, together the grace of childhood, together the service to obtain perfection, one is salvation, one is hope, and love undivided. Thus in Christ and in the Church there is no inequality based on race or ethnicity, social status or gender; for 'there is no longer any Jew and Greek, no slave and freeman, no man and woman; for you are all one in Christ Jesus (Gal 3:28; cf. Col 3:11)'.

The substantive similarity of these statements with the previously published Encyclical Letter from John XXIII, Pacem in terris (1963), concerning human rights as the norm and their application to women is unmistakable. Galations 3:28 (abolition of differences between men and women in Christ) is cited as the biblical basis for human rights. But although these programmatic declarations contain several important starting points and constitute the prerequisites for overcoming serious discrimination of women within the Church and their exclusion from all ordained ministries on the basis of the female gender, no reforms along these lines have been derived from them, nor have any even been pledged. At most a reform of the status of women in the laity appears to have been contemplated by the Council Fathers, although this has yet to be spelled out in any detail: "Since today women are exercising an ever more active function in the entire life of society, it is of great importance that they also participate increasingly in the different areas of the apostolate of the church" (decree regarding the lay apostolate Apostolicam Actuositatem, No. 9).

All this clearly illustrates that, although the Second Vatican Council achieved a 'reconciliation' of Catholicism with the democratic, liberal principles of secular society, it at the same time excluded the 'interior realm' of the church from these principles. Thus, statements by the Council advocate support for the civil rights of women, but not reform of their position in the ecclesiastical sphere,[37] as women conceived as equal members of the Church – with claim to full recogni-

---

[37] Thus notes Radford Ruether (see Note 32), p. 262.

tion of their personal dignity as human beings and Christians and to unrestricted equality in the Church – was beyond the sphere of thinking and conception of almost all Council Fathers. This is also emphatically revealed by the language and metaphors used in Council documents in a manner unbearable to feminist sensibilities. Reference is made to "Sons of the Church" and "brethren", when the focus should be on all members of the Church, women and men; other formulations include "acceptance in the Son's place" and "Sons of God" (e.g. LG nos. 2, 3, 11, 14, etc.): "The Christian man, having become wedded to the image of the Son, who is the first-born among many brothers, receives the 'first-birth gifts of the Spirit' ... Christ has risen from the dead, has abolished death by His death, and has given us life so that we, Sons in the Son, may call out in the Spirit: Abba, Father!" (GS No. 22). In only very few instances was this vision of the salvation of human beings, presented "as the drama of a purely male world[38]", even remotely transcended and the concrete concerns of women, their sisters, mentioned in a few statements by individual bishops[39]. Deserving special note in this context is the written intervention by Archbishop Paul Hallinan (Atlanta, U.S.) in the Council, which, however, was not submitted until October 1965, during the 4th session: He demanded not only that women be admitted to the offices of lecturer and acolyte in worship, but that the office of deacon also be opened to women; he furthermore argued that women should be involved in theological teaching as well as in the revision of *Codex Iuris Canonici*[40]. Despite the great publicity associated with it, his initiative was no longer capable of achieving any success – the end of the Council was drawing near. His initiative can be directly traced back to Council adviser Placidus Jordan, who had disseminated the (aforementioned) Council submissions by women collected in the American Bishops' Conference[41]. In the past, however, his intervention would not even have been possible because "the debate over the active participation of women in worship, especially their service in the diaconate and priesthood, only developed over the course of the Council, not least thanks to several private Council submissions", which were collectively

---

[38] Very aptly Heinzelmann, Sisters (see Note 29), 32.
[39] Worth mentioning are the interventions by Bishops Coderre (Quebec, Canada), Frotz (Cologne, Germany), Malula (Leopoldville, Congo), which are documented by Heinzelmann, Schwestern (see note 29), pp. 71 – 79.
[40] See Heinzelmann, Schwestern (cf. Note 29), pp. 78f (wording of the intervention) and in its entirety. (This book is as far as I am aware the only publication from the period immediately after the Council documenting and drawing up a balance sheet on the results of the Council from a feminist perspective.); cf. also: ibid., Diskriminierung (cf. Note 9), p. 138.
[41] For further details and the intervention of Archbishop Hallinan, cf.: Heinzelmann: Diskriminierung (cf. Note 9), p. 138; ibid.: Schwestern (cf. Note 29), p. 20. Due to the conclusion of the debate, the intervention could no longer be presented, but it belongs to the Council acts.

published in the book 'Wir schweigen nicht mehr! – Frauen äussern sich zum 2. Vatikanischen Konzil', "causing quite a stir all over the world".[42]

Reactions to 'We Won't Keep Silence Any Longer!'

So it was that the topic of 'women and Church' perceptively gained attention in the last phase of the Council. Several articles were published supporting this feminist initiative in response to the book "We Won't Keep Silence Any Longer!"[43]. This was the situation when restorative circles in the Vatican began marshalling their forces for a counter-offensive against the efforts to open up the priesthood to women. With an explicit reference to "We Won't Keep Silence Any Longer!", but characteristically enough without any additional bibliographical information, *Osservatore Romano* published a whole series of articles on the subject of *La donna e il Sacerdozio* before the end of the Council[44]. These were authored by the traditionalist Franciscan Father Gino Concetti. His introductory remarks (which are still very revealing today) clearly show that the movement to allow ordination of women was not only being observed very closely and warily by the Vatican – it was also condemned as errant in a degrading manner: "The atmosphere of fervent efforts surrounding the run-up to the Second Vatican Council and accompanying it has seen a number of additional initiatives, including those seeking to draw the attention of the church hierarchy to a movement to extend the office of priesthood to women. (...) The subject has recently been taken up by Protestants and Protestant circles. Since 1948 it has been the subject of enquiries by a commission of experts of the World Council of Churches." Concetti then goes on to cite a publication by the World Council of Churches "Zur Frage der Ordination der Frau" from 1964, characterizing it as worthless due to its allegedly untenable grounds. Concetti continues: "Analogous attempts have emanated from certain groups of Catholic women who have cast their votes and submitted resolutions to the preparatory commission of the Vatican Council. Recently these same groups have published a book in German and English with the revealing title 'We Won't Keep Silence Any Longer!' Some theologians have not been averse to joining the female choir with more or less restrained statements. There have even been some qualified theologians among them – as if the church had not issued a definitive and unalterable answer to resolve the matter back in the early years of Christianity ... ". The sharp rebuff of the call to open the priesthood to women that then

---

[42] G. Heinzelmann, Schwestern (cf. Note 29), p. 20.
[43] For sources cf.: Heinzelmann: Diskriminierung (cf. Note 9), p. 131 with Note 35; special mention should be made here to the supporting article by Renè J.A. van Eyden in Dutch journals.
[44] Osservatore Romano from 8, 9, 11 and 12 November 1965; German translation of the article in Heinzelmann, Schwestern (cf. Note 29), pp. 89 – 101. Ibid., 23 f, critical comments on the article.

followed was based on a collection of traditional texts compiled without any critical analysis of contemporary history and in which a demand was forwarded for the subordination of women to men, which, according to Concetti, is ultimately to be traced back to a command given by Jesus Christ. He concludes that: "Christ could have chosen women if he had wanted to (...) in order to elevate them to the office of priest. He refrained from doing this, not out of respect for a societal tradition, but rather out of respect for the order of creation and the plan of salvation, both of which necessitate the dominion of man: all the way back to the first human being, Adam (who Concetti understood to mean a man), and to the new Christ.[45]

The article by Concetti "provoked the fiercest of discussions among Council Fathers... Monsignor George Higgins of the Bishop's central office in the U.S. rightly rectified the widespread view that the Osservatore Romano was a semi-official statement, pointing out that the Osservatore Romano was not in charge of issuing church doctrine. (...) Efforts were made within the Osservatore Romano to issue a rejoinder, but these were suppressed ... ". Although the said article, written by a journalist about 'women at the Council', was finally published in the German edition of the Osservatore, this was only after being completely dismembered: Any and all mention of the book published by Gertrud Heinzelmann, "We Won't Keep Silence Any Longer!" and the priesthood of women was deleted.[46]

But not only male theologians adopted a sharply opposing position toward the ordination of women – so did women themselves, such as the writer Ida Friederike Görres in her article "Über die Weihe von Frauen zu Priesterinnen".[47] In this article, she unleashes a virtual diatribe against women: Women's ambitious, power-seeking nature makes them unsuitable for the office of priesthood, which is reserved solely for men as the identical gender serving as symbol of the 'bridegroom' Christ. J.Th. Münch finally succeeded – albeit in the face of major difficulties – in having a well-founded rejoinder published in the magazine *"Der christliche Sonntag"*.[48] The opposing positions of the two authors sparked a lively debate.[49]

Contrary to expectations, however, not only traditionalist women, but also women trained in theology, adopted a contrary position at the time – although

---

[45] Cited in Heinzelmann, Schwestern (cf. footnote 29), 99.
[46] Heinzelmann, Diskriminierung (cf. Note 9), pp. 139f (additional information on the case is provided here).
[47] Der christliche Sonntag (CS) from 20 June 1965. The article authored by I.F. Görres also appeared as an English translation in Herder Correspondence, July 1966, Vol. 3 no. 7, but without the reply of J.Th. Münch (Note 48).
[48] "Sollen die Frauen in der Kirche schweigen?" (CS from 15 August 1965) and "Katholische Priesterinnen?" (CS from 10 October 1965).
[49] For more information, see: Heinzelmann, Diskriminierung (see Note 9), p. 132.

in limited numbers and for other motives; for example Elisabeth Gössmann.[50] As far back as in her book "*Das Bild der Frau heute*", published in 1962,[51] she had remarked: "Rational women who have a correct understanding of their membership in the People of God would never even begin to imagine that they were missing something or that they were running up against a barrier because they cannot receive the sacrament of ordination".[52] In a later essay entitled "Das Ringen der Frau um ihr Selbstverständnis" (1964), however,[53] she tempered this statement, limiting it to women working in the area of pastoral care and catechetics, "who would always be reminded of their painful exclusion through the proximity of their work to those holding ecclesiastical office". She does not draw any conclusions regarding women's ordination from this, however. In a retrospective look, G. Heinzelmann[54] commented on what was in her view a contradictory standpoint (which was widespread in the 1960s) as follows: "Although she recognizes none of the common reasons cited opposing women's ordination as historically or exegetically unassailable, she nevertheless continues to argue for keeping women in the laity 'so that they can fully develop their potential for the first time in the history of the Church'. With regard to her "career plans", the "petition calling for equality in principle came for her at an extremely untimely moment."[55]

The discussion in the post-conciliar period

In the post-conciliar phase, the debate over the topic of 'women and the church' finally reached universities. But it was precisely here that years of hard pioneering work were needed to prepare the ground for a certain acceptance of reform of

---

[50] See also Heinzelmann, Diskriminierung, pp. 132 – 135, from which the following bibliographical references and quotations are taken.
[51] Haus der katholischen Frauen, Verlagsabteilung, Düsseldorf 1962.
[52] Elisabeth Gössmann, Bild der Frauen (see footnote 51), p. 111 Footnote 24.
[53] Die Frau im Aufbruch der Kirche, Theologische Fragen heute, Vol. 5 (Munich: Max Hueber Verlag 1964), p. 119.
[54] Heinzelmann, Diskriminierung (see footnote 9), p. 133.
[55] While E. Gössmann was still sharply criticizing the pioneering work of women in 1968 (Die Frau als Priester?, in: Concilium 4 [1968] pp. 288 – 293): "Wir schweigen nicht länger!" (1964) (here: p. 291) in disregard of the fact that the commitment to women's ordination is an effort to obtain recognition of priestly offices for women and thus at the same time the fundamental right of free choice of profession for women in the Church – she, on the basis of in-depth research on the history of discrimination against women, changed her attitude cf. *inter alia* on this point: Äußerungen zum Frauenpriestertum in der christlichen Tradition, in: Elisabeth Gössmann / Dietmar Bader (ed.), Warum keine Ordination der Frau? Unterschiedliche Einstellungen in den christlichen Kirchen. Munich – Zurich 1987, pp. 9 – 25 ("It is the responsibility of today's theology as the current stalwart of tradition to draw attention to the fact that the assumptions upon which the exclusion of women from the priesthood is based are untenable. Any conclusion drawn, no matter how correctly, based on false assumptions, however, remains as erroneous as the conclusion itself." ibid., p. 23).

the status of women in the church. As an example of the atmosphere reigning at Catholic theological faculties in the early 1960s, it is worthwhile having a glance at the situation at the Faculty of Catholic Theology at the University of Münster (Germany): Only men were working on the teaching staff, and all of them were priests. In their lectures, they almost without exception propagated a completely outdated image of women: the woman as a "background figure", unfit for the realm of politics, natural sciences, and especially for the priesthood and the "pulpit". Biblical texts, according to which women are merely "the reflection of man" (cf. 1 Corinthians 11:7) and should "be taught in complete subordination" (cf. 1 Timothy 2:12), were taken at face value and touted as a "God-given order". Marriage and consecrated virginity were offered as career alternatives for women in lectures in dogmatics. As students, men had a much wider latitude of choice: The entire ecclesiastical sphere of authority was open to them as an unquestioned matter of course.

As far back as the beginning of the 1960s, the Diplom theologian Iris Müller, at that time still a doctoral student, publicly protested against these discriminatory opinions that were being promulgated in lectures and courses. As a converted theologian (studying to become pastor) who had come from the Protestant Church, she recognized the backwardness and misogyny of the university atmosphere shaped by official Roman Catholic Church policy much more clearly than Catholic women, accustomed as they were to falling in line. Looking back, she recalls: "What I heard in lectures on the value of women (...) was appalling. So I approached the professor of ecumenical theology at the time (...) . His response to my question as to why women cannot be ordained in the Catholic Church shocked me deeply. He held that "[s]ince a man cannot give birth to children, he has the privilege of stepping up to the altar as compensation, whereas a woman has the privilege of motherhood."[56] These and other arguments were of course not able to persuade Iris Müller, and only served to strengthen her opposition to the anti-female structure of the Church cloaked in religion. Her open and honest criticism, however, had profound implications for her professional career. She was threatened with loss of her scholarship for example, which as a refugee from East Germany she was keenly dependent on[57]. In such a situation, she could not expect solidarity from other Catholic theology students.

As colleague and friend of Iris Müller, I (that is, Ida Raming) witnessed the professional and spiritual duress she was subjected to. I could relate to these spe-

---

[56] I. Raming et al. (ed.), Priesterin (cf. Note 4), pp. 49f.
[57] Ibid., pp. 47 – 51. For a more detailed description of the significant negative repercussions of this repression for professional careers, c.f: Gerburgis Feld, Dagmar Henze, Claudia Janssen (Eds.), Wie wir wurden, was wir sind. Gespräche mit feministischen Theologinnen der ersten Generation. Gütersloh 1998, pp. 60 – 67, here: pp. 62f.

cific consequences of oppression of women in the Roman Catholic Church; after all, I myself had suffered from the lack of freedom for women in my life up until then, which had been dominated by Church norms – suffering from the barring of women from ordained ministries merely because of their female gender![58] As a result of this personal experience as a woman in the Roman Catholic Church, I came to see it as my life task to work to overcome Church structures hostile to women, manifested above all in the exclusion of women from the ordained ministry.

This being my objective, I succeeded, even before the conclusion of the Second Vatican Council, in convincing the Ordinarius for Canon Law and Church Legal History at the time, DDr. Peter-Josef Kessler, to supervise my dissertation on the exclusion of women from the priesthood and its legal-historical as well as dogmatic foundations. That was an extremely rare occurrence at that time. Professors – with very few exceptions – tended to be more inclined to demonstrating their loyalty to Church teachings. In my study, I was only able to rely on a few relevant works. Only one critical, typewritten dissertation on women and the priesthood was available. The work had been written by Haye van der Meer SJ under the direction of Karl Rahner. If at all, Karl Rahner wanted to allow publication of this work only after the Council in order to avoid repression by Church authorities.[59] The dissertation was finally published in 1969 under the title *"Priestertum der Frau? Eine theologiegeschichtliche Untersuchung"*[60]. It critically explores the exegetical, historical and dogmatic reasons for the exclusion of women from the priesthood, arriving at the conclusion that none of the traditional arguments are tenable and therefore cannot be used to justify an ius divinum. Van der Meer does not unequivocally advocate women's access to the priesthood, however, instead leaving the question open. It is significant that he adopts an ambivalent, even disparaging attitude towards women who specifically aspire to the priesthood.[61]

In the winter semester of 1969/70, my dissertation was accepted by the Theological Faculty at the University of Münster and published in 1973 under the title *"Der Ausschluß der Frau vom priesterlichen Amt – Gottgewollte Tradition oder Diskriminierung?"*[62] It proved to be extremely difficult to get the work pub-

---

[58] For more details cf.: Raming et al. (Ed.), Priesterin (cf. Note 4), pp. 78 – 87.

[59] On this, K. Rahner characteristically enough remarked: "It's a shame to simply have to put some things on ice." In: Herlinde Pissarek-Hudelist, Die Bedeutung der Sakramententheologie Karl Rahners für die Diskussion um das Priestertum der Frau, in: Herbert Vorgrimler (Ed.), Wagnis Theologie, Freiburg 1979, p. 427, with Note 38, cf. also Heinzelmann, Diskriminierung (cf. footnote 9), p. 128.

[60] Quaestiones disputatae, 42, Freiburg 1969. The original title of the dissertation was: "Theologische Überlegungen über die Thesis: 'subiectum ordinationis est solus mas" (Innsbruck 1962).

[61] Cf. on this: Heinzelmann, Diskriminierung (see footnote 9), p. 147.

[62] The subtitle is: Eine rechtshistorisch-dogmatische Untersuchung der Grundlagen von Kanon 968 §1 des Codex Iuris Conanici, (Cologne-Vienna 1973).

lished, as Catholic publishers were unwilling. Finally, Böhlau-Verlag (Cologne – Vienna), a non-denominational publishing house, agreed to the task.

Compared to van der Meer's dissertation, my investigation produced more pointed results: Based on numerous sources from the early church and the Middle Ages (especially *Corpus Iuris Canonici*), I was able to demonstrate that the exclusion of women from the priesthood is based on the notion of the ontic and ethical inferiority of women. Certain biblical passages – such as Genesis 2 and 3 on the creation of the woman from the "rib" of man and her alleged original sin – and not least the history of their reception and impact by church fathers and in early church orders offered the foundations for this. In the dogmatic part of my dissertation I addressed the traditional understanding of the priesthood, whose allegedly necessary reservation for men is forwarded as an obstacle to the ordination of women. In contrast to this view, I was able to show that a conception of the presbyterate based on biblical statements regarding congregations and ministries is certainly open to active cooperation of women.

Obviously as a result of these unambiguous conclusions, both my dissertation in the years after its publication and the author herself were exposed to repeated attacks and repressions by anti-female and restorative church groupings, which have still had repercussions down to this very day. Moreover, attempts were made to suppress the work by maintaining a vigil of silence. These methods of suppression ultimately failed, however, as in the ensuing period there were several positive reactions to the dissertation in other countries.[63]

Both doctoral dissertations, from Haye van der Meer as well as the author's, were translated into English and published in the U.S,[64] a clear indication of the growing interest in this subject outside Europe.

In addition to these scholarly works (as well as those cited in the foregoing), additional works were published in Europe in the 1960s and early 1970s, inter alia by Elisabeth Schüssler, Tine Govaart-Halkes, Sr. Vincent E. Hannon, Mary Daly and Placidus Jordan.[65] These books, some of which were written in a "popular

---

[63] Among others by professors Yves Congar, René Metz (both in France) and Leonard Swidler (U.S.), also to whom substantial gratitude is due for publication of the dissertation in America.

[64] The work of H. van der Meer was published in 1973 (Temple University Press, Philadelphia), that of the author in 1976 (The Scarecrow Press, Metuchen, N.J.).

[65] Deserving mention here are *inter alia* Elisabeth Schüssler, *Der vergessene Partner. Grundlagen, Tatsachen und Möglichkeiten der beruflichen Mitarbeit der Frau in der Heilsorge der Kirche* (Düsseldorf: Patmos-Verlag 1964); Tine Govaart-Halkes, *Storm na de stilte. De plaats van den vrouw in de Kerk* (Utrecht: De Fontein 1964); German version: *Frau – Welt – Kirche. Wandlungen und Forderungen* (Graz: Styria Verlag 1966); Sr. Vincent E. Hannon, *The Question of Women and the Priesthood* (London: G. Chapman 1967); Mary Daly, *Frau und Sexus* (Olten: Walter-Verlag 1970); this is primarily a translation of the original American edition *The Church and the Second Sex* (London/Dublin/Melbourne: Geoffrey Chapman 1968); Placidus Jordan, *Die Töchter Gottes. Zum Thema Frau und Kirche* (Frankfurt a.M.: Josef Knecht-Verlag 1973).

science" style, reached further circles of the Catholic population. Even members of traditional Catholic women's associations were encouraged to question the traditional Church role model for women.

Synods on the position of women within the Church

The increasing dissemination of information about the disadvantaged situation of women in the Roman Catholic Church through the publications mentioned above as well as through other media (films and magazines) did not remain without effect on official church institutions. In the end, they also had to address the question of women in the church. In the post-Council phase, both Roman Catholic synods of bishops and numerous national synods took place in European (and non-European) countries, at which women's ordination always played a role as well.

As early as 1970, a majority of the participants in the Dutch Pastoral Council were in favor of ordination of women to the priesthood[66]. Key preparations for this in the Netherlands were made by the St. Willibrord Association. Early on, this group, made up of women and men, had backed the initiative at the Second Vatican Council for the ordination of women (diaconate and presbyterate) described in the foregoing, supporting it with publications.[67] Other national European synods were not quite as progressive as the Dutch Pastoral Council,[68] restricting themselves to advocating the diaconate for women. Thus, for example, the '1972' Pastoral Synod in Switzerland adopted a resolution in favor of the diaconate for women, advocating further studies on opening the priesthood up to women. Similar decisions were taken at the Joint Synod of Dioceses in the Federal Republic of Germany (1971 – 1975).

While all these activities advocating ordination of women were taking place in the scholarly field and at the synodal level, forces seeking to preserve the status quo were coalescing in the Roman Catholic Church.

Under the Pontificate of Paul VI, an official document opposing admission of women to the priesthood was published for the first time in 1976: the Dec-

---

Joan Morris, *Against Nature and God. The History of Women with Clerical Ordination and the Jurisdiction of Bishops*. London 1973 – Of the increasing number of journal articles, the following warrant mention *inter alia*: Josef Funk, *Klerikale Frauen?* In: Österreichisches Archiv für Kirchenrecht 14 (1963) pp. 271 – 290; René van Eyden, *Die Frau im Kirchenamt. Plädoyer für die Revision einer traditionellen Haltung*, in: Wort und Wahrheit 22 (1967) pp. 350 – 362; Jan Peters, *Die Frau im kirchlichen Dienst*, in: Concilium 4 (1968) pp. 293 – 299; Joan Brothers, *Frauen im kirchlichen Amt,* in: Concilium 8 (1972) pp. 760 – 766.

[66] Cf. Herder-Korrespondenz 24 (1970) pp. 57, 130.
[67] For example, the group was constantly compiling literature lists on the subject of "Women and the Church". This was led by above all René J.A. van Eyden and Katharina Halkes.
[68] Cf. the overview in: Raming, Frauenbewegung (cf. Note 6), pp. 41f.

laration of the Congregation for the Doctrine of the Faith *Inter insigniores*[69]. It provoked critical reactions worldwide, not only from Roman Catholic women's associations, but also in theological circles, and even from members of Vatican authorities (the Bible Commission and Secretariat for Christian Unity), as they felt that they had been ignored in the drafting of the document.

Under the pontificate of John Paul II, harsher pronouncements against the ordination of women followed: for example, the Apostolic Letter *Ordinatio Sacerdotalis* (1994) on ordination to the priesthood as a reserve of men; and the *Responsum ad dubium* (1995) from the Congregation for the Doctrine of Faith. In it, their Prefect, Joseph Cardinal Ratzinger, affirmed in 'response to the doubts concerning the doctrine contained in the Apostolic Letter *Ordinatio Sacerdotalis*' that the doctrine (on priestly ordination being reserved for men only) was of an infallible nature.[70]

In spite of the Vatican's increasingly severe tone over time, numerous pastoral forums and discussions have taken place at diocesan level in various European countries speaking out in favor of women's access to the diaconate and advocating a continuation of the discussion on the ordination of women (along the lines of ordination to the priesthood).[71]

Worldwide Networking of the Women's Ordination Movement[72]

In the awareness that women cannot push through reforms all on their own given the preeminence of the patriarchal-clerical hierarchy, several internal women's church organizations have formed in European countries, especially since the Second Vatican Council. Together with comparable associations or groups on other continents and countries in the international network *Women's Ordination Worldwide* (WOW), founded in 1996, these publicly advocate women's ordination and thus full equality of women in church matters.

---

[69] For more details cf. Raming, ibid., pp. 43 – 50.

[70] For the texts of the official Church documents as well as a critical analysis of these, see: Walter Groß (Ed.), Frauenordination. Stand der Diskussion in der katholischen Kirche, Munich 1996.

[71] For a detailed overview, cf.: Dorothea Reininger, Diakonat in der Einen Kirche, Ostfildern 1999, esp. pp. 50 – 55.

[72] The various European (and non-European) organisations are presented in: Raming et al. (ed.), Priesterin (cf. Note 4), pp. 237 – 247; for more cf.: Iris Müller, Ida Raming, Aufbruch aus männlichen 'Gottesordnungen'. Reformbestrebungen von Frauen in christlichen Kirchen und im Islam, Weinheim 1998, pp. 53 – 64. Most recently in detail – taking into account the reform initiatives emanating from the organizations – in: Raming: Frauen suchen Antworten. Reaktionen auf frauenfeindliche Blockaden, in: Orientierung 64 (2000) pp. 100 – 103; pp. 111 – 114.

Under the banner "The time is ripe! Women celebrate their calling to renewed priesthood in the Catholic Church", WOW held the First International Conference on Women's Ordination in Dublin/Ireland from 29 June to 1 July 2001.

About 350 female participants and 40 male participants had come from 26 countries and 5 continents; in 11 resolutions they expressed their determination to stand up to fight together for access of women in service to ordained ministries (diaconate and presbyterate) in the Roman Catholic Church and not to be subject to intimidation on the way to this goal by any Vatican repression or prohibitions.[73]

The Second International WOW Conference was held in Ottawa (Canada) from 22 to 24 July 2005. This time as well, many participants (about 400) from all over the world, among them representatives of different Christian denominations, gathered together under the slogan of "Breaking Silence, Breaking Bread: Christ Calls Women to Lead" at Carleton University. Even though the aim and objective of all the women present was to reform the position of women in the Roman Catholic Church, repression in the form of a definitive prohibition against ordination of women by the Church leadership was still clearly perceptible: The participants developed different strategies – on the one side forward-looking, more progressive and radical, and on the other more hesitant (e.g. limiting themselves to demanding that women be admitted to the diaconate). Members of the first group had already planned the first ordination '*contra legem*' in Canada after a long preparation for 25 July 2005 – i.e. immediately following the WOW conference. On that day, 5 women were ordained as deacons and 4 women as priests. This memorable celebration took place on a ship on the St. Lawrence River, attracting many congress participants who wanted to witness the event.

The ordination of women in Canada is the fifth of a total of six ordinations that have so far been carried out against existing church law (c. 1024). The first was the ordination of seven women as priests on 29 June 2002 on a Danube ship. Further ordinations followed on 26 June 2004, again on a ship on the Danube, for the first time in France on 2 July 2005, for the first time in Switzerland on 24 June 2006. On 31 July 2006 the first ordination in the USA took place on the Ohio River near Pittsburgh, where 12 women (4 for the diaconate and 8 as priests) were ordained. It is already evident now that additional ordinations of this nature will be taking place worldwide in the future.

With this procedure. the women involved bear witness to the fact that they want to pursue their service in the spiritual ministry, which is still suppressed by the ministers in charge to the detriment of the church despite all resistance. They also testify that they no longer want to accept the discriminatory law against

---

[73] For more information cf. below: Judith Stofer, "Die Mauer des Schweigens niederreißen", in: Publik- Forum Nr. 13 (2001) pp. 32f; conference reports, speeches in their entirety and resolutions, at: www.wow2001.org

women (c. 1024 CIC) and are proactively doing something about it. They are thus making a gesture of prophetic obedience to the holy spiritual power of God, which calls on women as well as men to assume the office of priestly service in the Church and to put an end to inhumane barriers.

Recalling as a form of resistance so that the early movement is not forgotten

Recalling the beginnings and gradual development of the women's ordination movement since the Second Vatican Council is not only a way to recall what has been forgotten and bring the previously unknown to light – it can also inspire new commitment in current reform work, especially with regard to overcoming anti-female structures of the Church.

Looking back over the more than 40 years that have passed since the beginning of the Council, it is evident that the initiative launched by a few women in Europe, motivated by their struggle for full recognition of the personal dignity of women and their religious calling to spiritual ministry in the church, has meanwhile become a worldwide movement for the ordination of women. Numerous reform groups and personalities as well as church synodic processes in various countries are leading the movement forward and maintaining it – despite all the repressive actions and 'definitive' proclamations and pronouncements against the ordination of women by the highest church authority.

There will therefore not be any reception or acceptance of Papal pronouncements against the ordination of women – all signs point to this. This is because the spiritual reality proclaimed in Galatians 3.27f will prove to be stronger than all these centralistic misogynous measures – taken without the involvement of the people of the church, not even by the bishops -: "All of you who were baptized into Christ have put on Christ. There are no more Jews and Greeks (Gentiles), no more slaves and free men, no more men and women; for all of you are 'one' in Christ Jesus."

The barriers between Jews and Gentiles and between free men and slaves have crumbled over time. In addition, recognition of human rights – irrespective of gender – has become enshrined as one of the basic principles of democratic states, and so is the right of women to choose their profession and their way of life freely. In contrast, responsible officials of the Roman Catholic Church, reacting against the "signs of the times" and to the detriment of the church, have acted with all their might to preserve traditional hierarchical-patriarchal structures, so that women in the Catholic Church remain unseen, disregarded, forgotten and void of rights. This situation is a tremendous disgrace and has led to an enormous loss of credibility for this ecclesial community. With its structure burdened by the sin of sexism, the Roman Catholic Church cannot claim to be the only and true Church of Christ.[74] Therefore all members willing to reform are challenged not only by the Roman Catholic, but also by the other, Christian churches: The task is to help the biblical pledge: "in Christ there is no man and woman" (Galatians 3.28) to achieve a breakthrough in the structures of the Christian churches without any caveats or restrictions, so that the last wall also falls in the power of the divine Spirit – that between men and women in the Roman Catholic Church. And this is at the same time an indispensable condition for the democratization and renewal of the Church.[75]

---

[74] Cf. Erklärung *Dominus Jesus*. Über die Einzigkeit und die Heilsuniversalität Jesu Christi und der Kirche. (Verlautbarungen des Apostolischen Stuhls, ed. Sekretariat der Deutschen Bischofskonferenz, Nr. 148) Bonn 2000, Nos. 16 and 17, p. 22.

[75] With this statement, I dispute and challenge the repeatedly forwarded assertion of Herbert Haag that through the ordination of women the 'two-estate structure' (clergy – laity) of the Church would be "further cemented", which is why he dismisses the demand for priestly ordination for women; cf. most recently in: Nur wer sich ändert, bleibt sich treu. Für eine neue Verfassung der katholischen Kirche, Freiburg – Basel – Vienna 2000, pp. 104f. In contrast, among others Christian Duquoc, Die Reform des Priesterstandes, in: H.J. Pottmeyer (Ed.), Rezeption (cf. footnote 1), pp. 369 – 383, views Vatican declarations against the ordination of women to be an "ideological justification of the status quo", a "blockade of the official Church" in relation to a reform of the priesthood (375). The "border that regulates access to the priesthood" (exclusion of women, exclusion of married persons) determines from the outset "the possible framework of reform"; for "no social and legal conditions may be introduced into the Roman Church that could negatively affect the hierarchical structure" (382).

III After the Second Vatican Council.

The new beginning of the church internally in the immediate wake of the Council is reflected in a multitude of publications: the demand for internal church reforms: e.g. ordination of women, right of lay people to have a say – and to take part in decision-making, etc.

A book authored by **Gertrud Heinzelmann: Die getrennten Schwestern. Frauen nach dem Konzil**, Zurich 1967, is particularly noteworthy in this context.

Among other things, it contains Council speeches given by the "Council Fathers" on the so-called "women's question". Her overall conclusion is, however: *"The aggiornamento has scarcely begun"* – a sobering statement.

Faced by this post-Conciliar awakening, the opposing side struck back in a restorative counter-movement seeking to destroy the Conciliar awakening:

Teaching documents opposing women's ordination:
Inter insigniores (1976)

In 1976, the first official letter of the Congregation for the Doctrine of the Faith was published under Pope Paul VI.

The core sentence it contains is: "For these reasons, the Congregation for the Doctrine of the Faith, in fulfilment of a mandate received from the Holy Father and in response to the declaration made by him in his letter of 30 November 1975, considers it its duty to reaffirm it":

"The church, out of fidelity to the example of her Lord, is not entitled to allow women to be ordained priests."

Numerous theologians opposed this, pointing out the untenability of the arguments in this teaching letter. Even the Pontifical Bible Commission questioned by the Congregation for the Doctrine of the Faith (in 1976) noted that in the New Testament there is no evidence for the exclusion of women from ordination. This answer was obviously not acceptable to the Congregation for the Doctrine of the Faith; thus it had the report of the Bible Commission "disappear" unpublished in "contemplation".

A basic documentary work from this period is: **Leonard Swidler and Arlene Swidler (eds.): *Women Priests. A Catholic Commentary on the Vatican Declaration.*** Paulist Press New York, Toronto... 1977

The editors, *Arlene* (now deceased) and *Leonard Swidler*, are among those theologians in the USA who advocated the ordination of women very early on.

But all these research results and objections were not accepted by the Congregation for the Doctrine of the Faith or by the Vatican Council, nor were they even afforded consideration.

In **1994** followed the **second teaching letter against the ordination of women** – the "Apostolic Letter" by Pope John Paul II: *Ordinatio Sacerdotalis (1994).*

The key sentences in this letter are:

4. "Although the doctrine of ordination to the priesthood only being reserved for men has been preserved both by the church's consistent and comprehensive tradition and has been taught with consistency by the Magisterium in recent documents, it is nevertheless considered in our time to be debatable in various places, or the church's decision not to admit women to this ordination is attributed merely disciplinary significance."

So, in order to remove any doubt about this important matter concerning the divine Constitution of the church itself, I declare, by virtue of my office of strengthening the brethren (cf. Luke 22:32), that the church has no authority whatsoever to ordain women priests, and that all the faithful of the church must finally abide by this decision".

This "definitive" letter also very soon aroused critical dissenting voices, e.g.
Walter Groß (ed.) Frauenordination. Stand der Diskussion in der katholischen Kirche. Erich Wewel Verlag, Munich 1996.

This is an important basic work on which several important theologians collaborated.

See also:

Anneliese Lissner: "Seid nicht so geduldig!" Warum der Kirche widersprochen werden muss. Einsiedeln / Benziger 1994

Furthermore:

Ida Raming. Endgültiges Nein zum Priestertum der Frau? Zum Apostolischen Schreiben Papst Johannes Pauls II. *Ordinatio Sacerdotalis** This article, "Endgültiges Nein... ", is published in: Orientierung 58 (1994) pp.190–193; then in slightly revised form in: I. Raming: Römisch-katholische Priesterinnen... LIT Publishing House 2013, pp. 84–90.

Final "no" to women in the priesthood?
The Apostolic Letter of Pope John Paul II
*Ordinatio Sacerdotalis**

According to the will of John Paul II, the Apostolic Letter *Ordinatio Sacerdotalis* of 22 May 1994[1] was intended to make a binding doctrinal decision rejecting admission of women to priestly ordination, to which "all the faithful of the church must finally abide by" (No. 4). The Pope resolutely rejected the view that the exclusion of women from priestly ordination was only of "disciplinary significance" and that this practice could continue to be an object of theological discussion. He opposed the mounting reservations being expressed regarding doctrinal statements on this subject – especially since the introduction of female ordination in the Anglican Church of England – with his Exhortation laying down the law to remove any "doubt concerning the important matter concerning the divine constitution of the church itself" (No. 4). But is something like this so easy to do this with a Papal decree?

The manifold critical reactions to the Pope's Exhortation to date clearly indicate that the decision by the Papal teaching authority necessarily runs up against limits and hence remains ineffectual, as it is based on theological notions and ideas and ways of thinking which by no means stand up to a scholarly theological examination. "Well-founded counterarguments to the position of the Magisterium regarding the ordination of women to the priesthood cannot be put to an end by the use of authority – no matter how massive it may be."[2] Nor will the official notes[3] to the Apostolic Letter, published in the "*Osservatore Romano*" (of 30/31 May 1994), which go considerably beyond it in terms of severity and remorselessness, be able to reverse the state of theological knowledge that has been achieved in the meantime.

Strengthening the binding nature?

The choice of words and intention of the official document presenting the ideas are striking and remarkable due to the fact that even more massive weight is assigned

---

[*] Published for the first time in: "*Orientierung*" 58 (1994), pp. 190–193; here in slightly revised form.

[1] German text in HK: 48 (1994) pp. 355f with explanatory notes in the "Osservatore Romano" (ibid. pp. 356–358); now also available as: Verlautbarungen des Apostolischen Stuhls Nr. 117, Bonn 1994 (together with the Declaration by the Congregation for the Doctrine of the Faith *Inter insigniores* of 15 October 1976).

[2] Ulrich Ruh, Lehramt im Abseits? in: HK 48 (1994) p. 327; cf. also Peter Hünermann, Schwerwiegende Bedenken. Eine Analyse des Apostolischen Schreibens "Ordinatio Sacerdotalis", in: HK 48 (1994) pp. 406–410.

[3] HK 48 (1994) pp. 356–358.

to their binding nature here than in the Apostolic Letter itself: "No one, then, not even the highest authority of the church, can disregard this doctrine (on ordination to the priesthood being reserved only for men – note of the author) without distorting the will and example of Christ himself as well as the events of revelation . . . ". Although it is admitted that the Apostolic Letter is "not a new dogmatic formulation", the Pope's decision is nevertheless ascribed a quasi-dogmatic character, in that it is described as "a doctrine that is certainly true",[4] which is beyond the realm of free theological debate and "always requires full and unconditional acceptance by the faithful". In order to lend this provision the appearance of almost a divine commandment, the author of *Erläuterungen* is not averse to using intimidation of conscience, stressing that "teaching the opposite (of the Pope's word – note of the author) would be tantamount to seducing the conscience (of the faithful) to commit errors" since the "declaration by the Pope" is an "act of listening to God's word and of obedience to the Lord along the path of truth".

Critical remarks on the production of evidence

In the face of such an almost inflationary use of metaphysically loaded terms (e.g. "eternal plan of God", "divine Constitution of the Church", the "events of revelation", "truth") characterizing the Apostolic Letter, but especially the explanatory notes, this automatically broaches the question of upon what this purportedly "definitively binding" doctrine is based.[5]

---

[4] In view of this formulation the assumption itself suggests that this is a paraphrase of the term "infallible", which is avoided in the Apostolic Letter, cf. Archbishop Weakland (Milwaukee/USA): "I note that the Holy Father has avoided the word 'infallible', in: Origins 24 (1994) No. 4, p. 55f. – The greater weight assigned to the binding nature of the message in the *Erläuterungen* in my opinion already presages the *Responsum ad dubium* (of 28 October 1995) of the Congregation for the Doctrine of the Faith published soon thereafter, in which it is declared that the doctrine contained in *Ordinatio Sacerdotalis* belongs to the canon of belief which is "infallibly" presented by the ecclesiastical Magisterium and therefore requires "final acceptance"; furthermore, it portends the Apostolic Letter *Ad tuendam fidem* (of 18 May 1998), AAS 90/1998, pp. 457–461.

[5] In the following discussion my arguments are based *inter alia* on: Karl Rahner, Priestertum der Frau? in: StdZ 102 (1977), pp. 291–301; Ruth Albrecht, Art. Apostle/Disciple, in: Wörterbuch der feministischen Theologie, Gütersloh 1991, 24–28; Ida Raming, "Die zwölf Apostel waren Männer . . . " Stereotype Einwände gegen die Frauenordination und ihre tieferen Ursachen, in: Orientierung 56 (1992), pp. 143–146; the following articles are also relevant: "Theologische Quartalschrift H.3/1993 on the topic of "women's ordination". Cf. also the statement by the Biblical Commission from 1976, which states that by a majority of 12 to 5 it had voted that the priesthood of women is not excluded on the basis of New Testament writings. The text of this opinion is provided in: Leonard and Arlene Swidler, Women Priests. New York 1977, pp. 338–346.

It is merely the fact (reported in the New Testament) that Jesus appointed only men to the group of the "Twelve" and that this practice of appointing only men as ministers was maintained by the apostles in the election of their colleagues and followers to office (no. 2). "This appointment," according to the Pope, "also included those persons who throughout the history of the church were supposed to continue appointing apostles, Christ (no. 2) The teaching on ordination to the priesthood, reserved only to men, was "both preserved by the church's consistent and comprehensive tradition and taught with consistency by the Magisterium in documents of the recent past" (n. 4). Summarizing his statements, the Pope draws the following conclusion: "that the church has no authority whatsoever to ordain women priests". (Number 4)

A detailed analysis of the arguments in *Ordinatio Sacerdotalis* (already presented in Inter insigniores [1976]) from "Scripture and Tradition," is contained in the article "Die Zwölf Apostel waren Männer" ("The Twelve Apostles were men... "), which we cite here.

Failure to respect recognized rules of interpretation

In several respects, in its treatment of the Bible, the Apostolic Letter deviates from the standards and rules published in 1993 in "The Interpretation of the Bible in the Church"[6]. Thus, the historical-critical method, which is considered indispensable, is not taken into account at all; on the contrary, the Apostolic Letter remains rooted in a fundamentalist interpretation, although this is emphatically rejected by the Biblical Commission. Furthermore, the Pope bases his decision on arguments *e silentio*, which "can never be sufficient for a firm and solid conclusion"[7]. Additional weaknesses in the argumentation of the Papal letter, which can only be mentioned here, concern the incorrect portrayal of the development of church offices as well as of church tradition...

Misogyny not overcome

It follows from all this that the reasons given in the Apostolic Letter for the exclusion of women from priestly ordination are all unfounded. To base a definitive decision having the force of law on such arguments, according to which half of all church members, women, are excluded from ordination and the priesthood as a result of their gender (cf. c.1024 CIC/83), is a monstrosity and a grave injustice,

---

[6] Cf. the German text in: Verlautbarungen des Apostolischen Stuhls Nr. 115, Bonn 1994; cf. Herbert Haag, Bilanz eines Jahrhunderts. Ein Lehrschreiben der Päpstlichen Bibelkommission: Orientierung 58 (1994), pp. 129–132; cf. also U. Ruh (cf. note 2), p. 327.

[7] H. Haag (cf. note 6), 131.

illustrating with unmistakable clarity to what extent women are at the mercy of patriarchal arbitrariness in the Roman Catholic Church. The theological proofs for the Apostolic Letter and other recent doctrinal writings to which the Pope explicitly refers (among others *Inter insigniores, Mulieris dignitatem*, Catechism of the Catholic Church No. 1577) are ultimately based on a misogyny that has yet to be overcome, which is manifested in women being at the disposal of the Church and assigned a dependent, subordinate role there.

Critical observers (in the USA) see a connection (in terms of time and content) between the Apostolic Letter *Ordinatio Sacerdotalis* and Vatican policy in the run-up to the International Conference on Population and Development (ICPD) held in Cairo; the Vatican's firm rejection of artificial birth control at the same time constituted an attack on the self-determination of women in the sexual sphere and opposition to the growing importance of women and their concerns at this conference.[8] In both cases the intention is to preserve and uphold patriarchal gender relations.

While this antiquated, unjust distribution between the roles of the sexes based on the exclusion of women from the priesthood in accordance with Vatican language is disguised[9] by the innocuous labels of "diversity" and "complementarity" of the sexes, or through mystified religious categories: "symbolic transparency of corporeality", bond to the "mystery of the incarnation" (in the context this can only mean: to the manhood of Christ!), "bond to the will of the Creator and the internal church bond to the will of the Redeemer" are built up and thus declared as indispensable.[10]

The demand for equality of women in the priesthood on the basis of their human dignity, on the other hand, is portrayed as an externalized, purely functional understanding of the priesthood in the sense of a position of power ("decision-making power") and is discredited as a disastrous path to the mere "functional equivalence of the sexes", to an "abstract, genderless human being" and thus rejected for this reason as well.[11]

Of course, such an approach completely disregards basic "fundamentals" requiring gender equality and thus equal access to church offices: the personal dig-

---

[8] Cf. the article by D. Von Drehle, Population Summit has Pope worried. Vatican fears Advocacy of reproductive Rights, in: The Washington Post from 16 June 1994.

[9] Besides many documents in Vatican pronouncements once again in: Address of John Paul II "Würde und Sendung der christlichen Frau", in: L'Osservatore Romano 24 (1994) no. 26 of 1 July 1994, p. 1f.

[10] Mentioned strikingly often in the explanatory article to the Apostolic Letter *Ordinatio Sacerdotalis* by Josef Ratzinger: "Die Kirche kann nicht machen, was sie will", in: Rheinischer Merkur No. 22 from 3 June 1994, p. 27 and p. 30; now as well, supplemented by an annotation apparatus, in: Internationale Katholische Zeitschrift 23 (1994), pp. 337–345.

[11] Cf. J. Ratzinger (see note 10), pp. 27 and 30.

nity of women, their being baptized and confirmed, their mystical union with Christ as a member of the church, the right to freely choose one's vocation (enshrined in CIC c. 219)[12], not least the promise expressed in Galatians 3.28 that "in Christ there is no male or female", lifting and abolishing the unchristian supremacy of men once and for all and therefore, characteristically enough, does not appear anywhere in the Papal Letter or the explanatory notes to it.

The need to turn away from the sin of sexism

For the church leadership, nothing less than turning away from the outdated assignment of gender roles and thus from the sin of patriarchalism is therefore a must if it does not want to ossify in the image of "old Adam" (Ephesians 4.22) and thus hold back and prevent the dawn of the Kingdom of God in the church. On the positive side, this means turning to what the Kingdom of God (according to Ephesians 4:24) means: "and to put on the new self, created to be like God in true righteousness and holiness" and (according to Galatians 3:27f): "For all of you who were baptized into Christ have clothed yourself with Christ. There is neither Jew nor Gentile, neither slave nor free, nor is there male and female, for you are all one in Christ Jesus."

Overcoming all domination of human beings by human beings, of women by men, will make the image of God and Christ shine out brightly in both genders, so that the Easter message of liberation and rebirth in Christ will at last also apply to women and they will no longer be cheated out of it.

For (Catholic) women this letter by the Pope should serve as an occasion to courageously and resolutely oppose any discrimination in defense of their gender, to demand full recognition of their status as individual human beings and their creation in God's own image as well as their religious vocation – including the priestly ministry – in the church. To use the words of John Paul II: "Women themselves are obliged to cooperate in order to gain respect for them as individuals, and they must not in any form compromise with that which is contrary to their dignity".[13] Commitment to full recognition of their personal dignity must indeed come from women themselves. But it must be left up to women themselves to decide what is contrary to their dignity, and it is not for men, not even the Pope, to decide for them and tell them what to do, as was indeed the case in his Apostolic Letter (*Ordinatio Sacerdotalis*, No. 3). This is because the Pope's reference here to Mary's unique service as "Mother of God and Mother of the Church", which nevertheless "was not given the same mandate as the apostles to serve as

---

[12] Cf: Ida Raming, Ungenutzte Chancen für Frauen im Kirchenrecht. Widersprüche im CIC/1983 und ihre Konsequenzen, in: Orientierung 58 (1994) 68–70.

[13] Address on the "Würde und Sendung der christlichen Frau" (cf. note 9), pp. 1f.

missionaries", is not suitable as proof that "the non-admission of a woman to priestly ordination cannot mean a diminishment of their dignity or any discrimination against them", – for Mary was subject to the same patriarchal laws as the other women of her people. Moreover, Mary's religious service and significance as the Mother of Jesus Christ, insofar as it is not misinterpreted and distorted by androcentrically shaped Mariology, does not in any way contradict the priesthood of women – on the contrary![14]

The Apostolic Letter *Ordinatio Sacerdotalis* definitely degrades women – their dignity and rights as members of the church are blatantly disregarded. This is a challenge for all Catholic women. They are called upon to fight for their liberation for the sake of their dignity. But the movement for the liberation of women requires the solidarity of men with a sense of justice if it is to be effective and bring about a fundamental renewal of the church.

The following article is also instructive:

Ida Raming
Immer härtere Schläge gegen die Frauenordination
("Ever harsher blows to women's ordination")

For any observer of current internal church events, the increasingly sharp reaction against the ordination of women – for that matter, against any audible reflection over the access of women to the priesthood – is quite plain to see. Only recently the Vatican (the Pope and representatives of the Curia) has provided several very revealing examples of this.

Remembering: Official Vatican documents opposing the ordination of women

With his Apostolic Letter *Ordinatio Sacerdotalis* (1994), Pope John Paul II put a resolute end to the ever louder discussions over the ordination of women, and this despite the declaration issued by the Congregation for the Doctrine of the Faith *Inter Insigniores* (1976), which for the first time spoke out against the ordination of women, by stating with the weight of his authority:

"Therefore, in order to remove any doubt about the important matter concerning the divine constitution of the church herself, I declare by virtue of my ministry of strengthening the brethren (cf. Luke 22:32) that the church has no authority to ordain women priests and that all the faithful must definitively abide by this decision" (OS no. 4).

The Congregation for the Doctrine of the Faith subsequently ascribed an "infallible nature" to this "definitive" doctrinal statement: The doctrine of the Apostolic Letter *Or-*

---

[14] On this, see Wolfgang Beinert, Dogmatische Überlegungen zum Thema Priestertum der Frau, in: Walter Groß (Ed.), Frauenordination. Stand der Diskussion in der katholischen Kirche, München 1996, pp. 64–82, here: pp. 76f (Wherever "theologians and mystics... have contemplated the Mother of Christ and her role in salvific history, the notion of a priesthood of Mary has almost forced itself upon them..."); furthermore: John Wijngaards, The Ordination of Women in the Catholic Church, London 2001, pp. 156–163.

dinatio Sacerdotalis, it was held, is part of the church's religious doctrine (*Responsum ad dubium*, 1995).

As is well known, Cardinal Ratzinger, Prefect of the Congregation for the Doctrine of the Faith at the time, was the main force inspiring these last two documents. But in the wake of this "definitive" doctrinal statement as well, the question as to women's access to the priesthood could not be completely silenced, as theologically untenable pronouncements do not automatically become true simply through constant repetition. Valid counter-arguments cannot be dismissed simply by asserting the weight of authority.

As is well known, the majority of the Pontifical Biblical Commission had already declared in 1976 that a ban on female priests could not be inferred from the NT, and that, furthermore, Christ's plan of salvation would not be overstepped or falsified by allowing the ordination of women. With its declaration *Inter Insigniores* (1976), the Congregation for the Doctrine of the Faith completely ignored this report by the Bible Commission, although it had previously commissioned the Bible Commission with an exegetical study on the question of the ordination of women. The Congregation for the Doctrine of the Faith, however, did not approve of the result of this investigation: it ignored the report and has kept it secret down to this very day!

This line was rigorously continued under former Cardinal Ratzinger, now Pope Benedict XVI.

Facts and examples that speak for themselves... The following examples, all from this year, 2011, illustrate this in all clarity:

In his book *Licht der Welt* – a conversation with Peter Seewald – the Pope emphasizes – with reference to his predecessor: "The formulation of John Paul II (one must add: *Ordinatio Sacerdotalis*, see above) is very important: The church has 'no authority whatsoever' to consecrate women. It is not that we say we do not want to, but rather: we cannot. The Lord provided the church a structure with the Twelve – and in their succession then with the bishops and presbyters, the priests. This structure of the church was not made by us, rather it was constituted by Him. To follow this is an act of obedience, an obedience that may be laborious in the present situation. But it is precisely this that is important for the church to show: We are not an arbitrary regime. We cannot do whatever we want. Rather, there is a will of the Lord for us to obey, even if this is laborious and difficult in this culture and civilization.

It is obvious: The Pope is entrenching himself behind Jesus and God to justify in theological terms his rejection of the ordination of women. But the truth of the matter is that he and the representatives of the Curia who surround him want to prevent women's access to the priesthood by any and all means and have no qualms about using Jesus and God as religious justification for this!

It has long since been shown that the Pope simply ignores basic historical research available: for example, the status of women in ancient Israel. (Women were excluded from public teaching in the synagogues, and in court they could not give public testimony. How should they then assume a preaching task in the apostolic ministry!?) At the same time, the development of ministry in the early church is completely ignored by the Pope: in the early church, there were indeed women serving as deacons, presbyters and missionary apostles, as New Testament research has long since demonstrated.

"We are not an arbitrary regime," says the Pope, "We cannot do whatever we want."

The following facts – all of which constitute repressive measures against the ordination of women – indicate who and where the actual "arbitrary regime" in our church is to be found.
- William Morris, since 1992 Bishop of Toowoomba (Australia), stated in in a pastoral letter in 2006 that, in view of the ever greater threat of a shortage of priests in his diocese, he would propose that the ordination of married men and women be contemplated. Thereupon the Vatican initiated an investigative procedure against him. Without any possibility to defend himself, Bishop Morris was suspended from his episcopal office by Pope Benedict in May 2011 (reported in detail in 'Kirche In' No. 6/2011). Not an arbitrary regime?!
  The Australian bishops, who in October 2011 began their "ad-limina" visit to the Vatican, declared – after several talks with Cardinals in the high Curia, among others with the head of the Congregation for the Doctrine of the Faith, Cardinal William Levada – that they now better understood the measures the Vatican had taken "to solve the difficulties with Bishop Morris". These difficulties concerned "not only questions of Church discipline, but also the binding teachings of the Church, such as the priesthood." "The unity of the Church and communion between the Pope and the other Bishops in the College of Bishops were at stake." Bishop Morris "could not agree to what was required to assure this unity." (see kath.net/Catholic News Agency).
  So the Australian bishops were "brought into line" at the Vatican! They abandoned their brother in office, who had dared to think for himself. – Not an arbitrary regime?!
- The Patriarch of Lisbon (Portugal), Cardinal Policarpo, stated in an interview (in June 2011) on the question of priestly ordination for women that in his opinion there was "no fundamental theological obstacle" to admitting women to priestly ordination in future as well. There is a fundamental equality among all members of the church. He also said that he did not advocate women in the priesthood only because of the "strong tradition" in the church, which restricts ordination to men.
- With the Apostolic Letter *Ordinatio Sacerdotalis*, Pope John Paul II "seemed" to have "decided the matter", judged Cardinal Policarpo, "but I think that the question of the ordination of women cannot be solved in this way (i.e. with such a document). I believe there is no fundamental obstacle." You could say that there is a tradition. Things had never been done differently. – There would be female priests, he continued, "as soon as God wills it", but at the moment it would be better not to raise the issue. [cath.net]
  Because of these statements the Cardinal was summoned to Castel Gandolfo. Tarcisio Bertone, the Cardinal Secretary of State, "washed his head" (according to cath.net).
- Shortly afterwards, the Cardinal declared in a letter (ZENIT.org): "The reactions to this interview (see above) forced me to look at the subject with greater scrutiny, and I reviewed whether I had given cause for these reactions, especially by not paying enough attention to the last statements of the Magisterium on this subject (see above!)".... "It would be painful for me if my words caused confusion in terms of our obedience to the church and the words of the Holy Father. I believe I have shown you that I am in perfect union with the Holy Father in the exercise of my ministry."

Rooted in the New Testament, he noted, the Christian priesthood had from the beginning been entrusted only to men. The most recent Magisterium of the Popes interpreted this uninterrupted tradition of consecrating only men "not only as a practice that can change under the action of the Holy Spirit, but as an expression of the mystery of the church itself, which we must accept in faith." "We are therefore invited," concluded the Cardinal, "to accept the teachings of the Holy Father with the humility of our faith." (ZENIT.org, 8 July 2011).

- Bishop Kapellari (Graz/Austria) felt compelled (in October 2011) – presumably under the pressure of the nuncio – to retract his statement: Only a council could decide to accept, to annul or to revoke the priesthood of women. He declared: "But a careful look at the sources of the Magisterium in their entirety shows that the doctrine of the impossibility of priestly ordination of women has finally been decided with such a magisterial weight, that even a council with its Pope could not change anything in this regard". (The Standard, 3 October 2011).- Not an arbitrary regime?!
- The Prefect of the Congregation for the Clergy, Cardinal Piacanza, declared (in September 2011): The non-admission of women to the priesthood in the Catholic Church is of a definitive nature. The view, sometimes described as an "evasion", to the effect that the Church's line in this matter was only of "relative finality", was absurd and lacked any foundation, he continued. The Curia Cardinal made reference in this context to the Apostolic Letter *Ordinatio Sacerdotalis* (of 22 May 1994). This document, he held, had finally clarified the question of women's priesthood.

"Unity of the Church" – enforced by coercion, manipulation and brainwashing

These numerous examples from a relatively short period of time speak for themselves: The exclusion of women from the priesthood is almost passed off as dogma, as a doctrine that is binding for all times – any deviation from it or even questioning of it is harshly punished.

With a doctrine thusly based on untenable exegetical and theological foundations and not least on discrimination against women, the Vatican (Pope and Curia) intends to "hold the Church together". A unity – a uniformity created by repression, by coercion. What does this have to do with the "unity" meant by Jesus?

This 'project of unity' will and must fail because it is directed against truth, justice and love: A few of the highest office-holders decree the exclusion of women from all ordained ministries for all time – they dispose over at least half of church members, the women, as they please, thereby assigning them to the lowest place in the hierarchical "order" created by them. It is patently obvious: The current Vatican church leadership (the Pope together with representatives of the Curia) is the real arbitrary regime! In violation of the message of Jesus Christ (cf. Galatians 3:27f) and counter to the 'signs of the times', it adheres to the patriarchal structure of the church with all its negative effects in an arbitrary and unswerving manner.

(Article published in: "Kirche In", 2011)

Effects of the "final" ban on the ordination of women (OS)

The effects of this ban on the Women's Ordination Movement were devastating – and to a certain extent still are, not least because *"Ordinatio Sacerdotalis"* has to a certain extent been "stylized" into an "infallible" Papal doctrine.

This act of doctrinal violence committed by John Paul II triggered a virtual *"rigor mortis"*: Professors of theology began avoiding the topic of women's ordination for fear of repression and sanctions.

Catholic women's associations (KDFB and kfd) in Germany also allowed themselves to be forced into silence, as they also had to fear punitive measures (of a financial and occupational nature – there is evidence of this). Their demands for reform were therefore limited to the diaconate of women.

It is probable that under the immediate predecessor of John Paul II, i.e. Albino Luciani, who gave himself the name John Paul I (1978) and only performed the office of the Papacy for 30 days – dying in the same year (1978) – such a devastating papal doctrinal decision, which contradicts the spirit of Jesus, would never have been taken. Albino Luciani sought a greater closeness to the people, expressly renouncing the *"plural majestatis"* and coronation with the tiara. The following words came from him: "God is Father, but even more He is Mother" (*È papà; più ancora è madre*).

In view of the "final" prohibition of the ordination of women by his successor John Paul II (in 1994), the order of the day was to search for:

Liberating paths of awakening and resistance.

What is to be done? Women and all people of good will are challenged to take up resistance against this arbitrary regime! In the meantime, numerous inner-church reform groups have dared a new beginning, relying on their conscience.

June 2002 – A liberating way out: *ordination contra legem* – women transgress the unjust law of their exclusion from ordination (CIC c. 1024:
"Holy Ordination is validly received only by a baptized man"); for: "an unjust law does not obligate" (*"lex iniusta non obligat"*).
Press statement on the occasion of the women's ordination in Austria (29 June 2002)

Several Catholic women from Austria and Germany decided to be ordained by a Catholic bishop. They thereupon informed the public of this decision, offering the following reasons:
- For 40 years now, i.e. since the beginning of the Second Vatican Council (1962–1965), women have rejected the reasons for their exclusion from church-ordained ministries with sound arguments. In the post-conciliar phase

until the present, numerous scholarly as well as popular science books and articles in favor of women's ordination have been published worldwide. The Vatican church leadership (Congregation for the Doctrine of Faith and the Pope) has so far ignored these research results, even when they came from the Pontifical Biblical Commission (cf. the Report by the Biblical Commission from 1976). Through repeated pronouncements (*Inter insigniores*, 1976, *Ordinatio Sacerdotalis*, 1994, *Responsum ad dubium*, 1995), it has instead cemented the exclusion of women from the priesthood and assigned this teaching the status of "quasi-dogma" ("This teaching requires final approval") .

- Women who feel a calling to the priesthood and want to practice this calling are therefore in a serious conflict of conscience: On the one hand, there is the unreformed position of the official church leadership – but on the other hand God calls them to the priestly service in the church. "The love of Christ compels them!" The women involved do not want to accept this unbearable tension and are therefore trying to find ways out.
- Since all experience shows that pursuing a path of argumentation does not hold out any prospects for a change in things, women have decided to strive for an *ordination contra legem* (c. 1024 CIC). This is because a change in the legal status of women in the Roman Catholic Church is not to be expected in the foreseeable future in view of its hierarchical and centralistic structure: As is well known, in a council that could decide on the question of the admission of women to ordained offices, only bishops (i.e. exclusively men!) have voting rights, and in the past the majority of these bishops have proved to be exceptionally submissive to the Pope and the teaching authority.
- Women are aware that by taking this step they are violating existing church law as well as a doctrine of the Church teaching authority. But: This law ("Holy Ordination is validly received only by a baptized man", c. 1024) as well as the church doctrine upon which it is based exhibit a serious disregard for the individual or human dignity of women and their Christian being. Baptism and confirmation of women is ignored, and the validity of ordination is subject to the proviso of the male gender!

Law c. 1024 as well as the doctrine on which it is based thus stand in blatant contradiction to the godlike image of women (Gen I:27), to the teaching of the Second Vatican Council (Lumen Gentium No. 32 and others) as well as to Galatians 3:27f, which says: "All of you who were baptized into Christ have put on Christ. There are no longer Jews and Greeks/ Gentiles, no longer slaves and free, no longer 'male and female', for you are all 'one' in Christ Jesus." Baptism – but not the male gender – is already emphasized by medieval canonists/theologians as a basic prerequisite for the validity of ordination ("... post baptismum quilibet potest ordinari") .

- So both the doctrine of the exclusion of women from ordained ministries and the law resulting from it (c. 1024 CIC) contain a false doctrine (heresy), which women in the Roman Catholic Church no longer want to be victims of.
- The women involved in 'illegal' ordination thus also understand their act as a clear prophetic sign of protest against the discriminatory teaching and laws against women that men of the Church have imposed on women and that is seriously damaging the Roman Catholic Church and its credibility in the eyes of the entire world:
- spiritual vocations of women as given by God to build and renew the church (cf. Ephesians 4:8,10–12) is being suppressed by church law (c. 1024). In view of the dire shortage of manpower afflicting the clergy (merging of several parishes due to the lack of priests and a reduced number of celebrations of the Eucharist, etc.), this is unjustifiable. Through their actions, the women involved want to pay tribute to the free work of the Divine Spiritual Power, which is given to everyone as She wills it (cf. 1 Corinthians 12:11), thus opening up new prospects for the future of the Roman Catholic Church: In agreement with the Bishops who ordained them, they wish to be strengthened and equipped through ordination for the following tasks, among others: pastoral support for people, especially women (groups), who have become alienated and estranged from the church: They urgently need spiritual sisters in ministry! Furthermore: Development and/or pastoral care of house churches or house communities. In addition, they want to be available for pastoral service to people whenever and wherever it is desired.
- The women engaging in this act consider themselves to be following Jesus, who broke laws established by the hierarchical religious authority of his time and religion (e.g. rules regarding Sabbath and purity ...). In his view, this did not constitute arbitrariness. Instead, he was acting based on the knowledge that people are not there to obey unjust, inhumane norms and laws, but rather that the laws of a religion should serve the people (cf. Mark 2:27 and others).
- Through their actions (*contra legem*) the women involved intend to call on the church officials in charge to finally respect the spiritual vocations of women to the ordained ministries and to give them sufficient space in the teaching, law and practice of the church.
- It is not the women who in view of the hardening of the church leadership feel compelled to act "*contra legem*" that deserve criticism, but rather the church officials in charge who brought about this dire need for action through their conduct.

On Easter morning, courageous disciples, *Mary Magdalena* and other women, went to the tomb of Jesus – out of faithfulness to their Master. The stone in front of the tomb was rolled away – they were the first to behold the risen Lord and thus became heralds of the Easter message.

Trusting in the power of the risen Christ, committed women today also want to pave a new path to their ordination and help roll away the heavy stone of discrimination which lies blocking the path of women in the Catholic Church. As womenpriests, they want to stand up and work for a church in which people, regardless of gender and race, can live together in justice and freedom and serve God in this manner.

The group of women commend themselves and their daring step to the goodness of God and the intercession of all the saints, especially the Mother of Jesus and *St. Theresa of Lisieux*, who was declared a teacher of the Church (*doctor Ecclesiae universalis*) in 1997. She said of herself, "*I feel called to the priesthood!*"

In June 2002
For the group of candidates for ordination:
Dr. theol. Iris Müller and *Dr. theol. Ida Raming*
(published in: I. Raming: Roman Catholic Priestesses, LIT Verlag 2013, 114–117)

In the following: Detailed presentation and grounds for our approach:
"Pioneers pave the way... The first public ordination "*contra legem*" (2002). [Source: I. Raming: Römisch-katholische Priesterinnen (2013), pp. 24–31, LIT Verlag 2013].

Women pioneer the way...
First public ordination '*contra legem*'

In this desolate situation, which has now been ongoing for decades, some women from Austria and Germany sought and found a way out of the impasse. After more than 40 years of struggling verbally and in publications for access to the diaconate and presbyterate – since the Second Vatican Council (1962–1965) – to which the Vatican church leadership has obstinately reacted with an ever more recalcitrant "No", these women recognized that the problem of women's ordination can unfortunately not be solved through the system itself, e.g. in the form of a "dialogue" with leading Church officeholders.

The long history of discrimination against women, which is by no means a thing of the past, and the powerlessness of women in the Catholic Church stand like an insurmountable wall. Women who feel a calling for the priestly ministry face the alternatives of either accepting without challenge the Church doctrine of excluding women from the priesthood with all the far-reaching consequences of such – or of forming resistance against Church teachings and the Church leadership.

So it was that seven women from Austria and Germany decided in 2002 to take action to resist existing church law (c. 1024) and the doctrine on which it is based, i.e. to administer *ordination contra legem*.

Precursor of the movement

We, the seven women ("the Danube Seven", as they are known in English-speaking countries), were aware that we were not the first to take this extraordinary path. There had been important forerunners whom we take delight in remembering and whom we recognize for their efforts: *Felix Davidek* (who died in 1988), one of the bishops of the underground church in the former Czechoslovakia, ordained women to the diaconate and priesthood as far back as 1970 – in contravention of existing church law. Based on a thorough knowledge of church history, he came to the conclusion that admission of women to ordained ministries will not at the same time be accepted by the members of the church in their entirety: "It must be someone who passes on what is only gradually maturing among the majority of humanity"[1]. For him, it was a matter of conscience to actively work for the ordination of womenpriests, as he was deeply convinced that there are women who – just like men – feel a calling to the priestly ministry – a calling that deserves recognition. He regarded the question of women's ordination as a "sign of the times"; and therefore did not hesitate to use the 'Kairos' – the opportunity of the moment – and make women's ordination a reality. He knew from experience:

"New things are not welcomed with open arms. If we want something new to be accepted, we must first create a fait acompli"[2].

The approach adopted by the seven women differed of course from that in the Czech underground church in that the ordination of the women performed by F. Davidek and other bishops was kept secret at first. This was necessary under the circumstances of the time, i.e. under the Soviet dictatorship.

On the other hand, the decision to move into the public sphere in the ordination of the 7 women on 29 June 2002 – under different historical circumstances – was only logical. (Our ordination as deaconesses had already taken place a few months earlier in private rooms). Through the public ordination to priesthood, the attention of "spectators" was decidedly focused on continuing discrimination against women in the Roman Catholic Church. Many people only learned through our public actions that there is still a law in Catholic Church law today (CIC1024)

---

[1] P. Sepp: Geheime Weihen. Die Frauen in der verborgenen tschechoslowakischen Kirche Koinótes. Ostfildern: Schwabenverlag 2004, p. 56
[2] Cf. M.Th. Winter: Out of the Depths. The Story of Ludmila Javorova, Ordained Roman Catholic Priest. New York: Crossroad, p. 125 (translation into German: I. Raming).

which excludes women from all ordained ministries solely on the basis of their gender. Following their spiritual calling, the seven women had themselves ordained, flying in the face of ecclesiastical law excluding them, thereby setting a prophetic sign before the eyes of the entire world – a sign that spiritual callings to church office cannot be suppressed by a law established by men. We cited a biblical verse saying: "One must obey God more than men" (Acts 5:29) as well as the actions of Jesus, who transgressed inhumane laws, thereby adopting unmistakable words:
"The Sabbath is there for the sake of man, not man for the sake of Sabbath" (Mk 2:27).

The women set a prophetic sign:
- that God calls women as priests: 'God's spiritual power is given to each one according to Her will' (1 Corinthians 12:11);
- that the callings of women must be recognized – so as to build and strengthen communities and to renew the Church;
- that the message of Jesus Christ is being turned into a reality: "All of you who were baptized into Christ have put on Christ. There is no more ... man and woman, for you are all 'one' in Christ Jesus" (Galatians 3:27f). (See the press release from 2002 on our ordination).

Reactions to our ordination

Our ordination provoked a strong reaction in the media, both before and after the event. Even today many people recall this unprecedented occasion ...

Immediately before our ordination, two articles adopting very different perspectives appeared in Publik-Forum (No. 11/2002, p. 50f); these articles are still relevant and informative today:

1. "This act cements the old clergy-based Church – in the New Testament there are no consecrated persons" (author: Prof. Norbert Scholl)
2. "Only action can be effective in the face of the opposition from Rome. Catholics need a culture of active disobedience. The ordination of priests is a beginning" (author: Peter Rosien, then editor-in-chief of Publik-Forum)

Which of the two authors correctly assessed the situation at the time?

Regarding 1) Norbert Scholl's line of argumentation: "The New Testament does not make mention either of any consecrated persons or any separate places of worship, ... Sacrificial acts ...

The idea of the Church being different from the other members of the congregation, a "spiritual state" which is endowed with the special sacramental "grace of consecration", with a qualified claim to leadership and healing authority, cannot be justified on the basis of the New Testament. In view of the return to the basic ideas of Jesus and original church practice taking place today, I regard the striving for a "priestly ordination" in the traditional sense by a bishop in apostolic succession as an expression of a structurally conservative way of thinking".

What can we say by way of response to this?

We, the 7 women, have admittedly "fallen into the fold" in the sense of current tradition of ordination. But what were our reasons for this?

- We wanted to set a prophetic as well as a political sign in the Church. An ordination, e.g. performed by members of a congregation, would not have had any ecclesiastical significance and would not have attracted any attention, neither among Church members nor among the hierarchy in the Vatican.
- Women who feel called to the diaconate and priesthood, after having examined their vocation, have in principle the right to ordination according to the rules in force, as men are entitled to.
- We therefore sought a Bishop who was validly ordained and willing to ordain women for the sake of the necessary renewal of the church; and we found such a Bishop (as well as another whose name we shall not disclose) (see the testimony of Bishop R. Braschi[3] and the testimony about him from René v. Eyden, Dr. theol.).

Although we were ordained according to "traditional rites", we had already arranged for a distinct, forward-looking difference to set off our 2002 ordination: The seven women cited a particular Bible verse in their ordination: *"One must obey God more than men"* (Acts 5:29). This public testimony is recorded in the notarial deed of ordination. The women therefore made no promise of obedience to the ordaining bishop.

This is a very significant difference compared to traditional ordinations, however, in which, as is well known, obedience to the bishop is pledged.

This is because we were aware of the calamity caused by the pledge of obedience taken by the clergy in our church, for it is precisely this vow that is behind the incapacity of the official church to reform.

In addition, some of the seven women were married.

So we already took two important reform steps which have yet to be taken in the Roman Catholic Church at our ordination.

Peter Rosien, a Protestant (!), correctly recognized this in his observations. He wrote:

"The only thing that could fundamentally unsettle the Curia would be mass signals of active disobedience. Seen in this light, the planned ordination of women-priests is a delicate little seedling that could grow into a forest of disobe-

---

[3] W. Ertel and G. Forster (ed.): "Wir sind Priesterinnen". Aus aktuellem Anlass: Die Weihe von Frauen 2002, Düsseldorf 2002, pp. 85–88 The testimony of v. Eyden is available as Ms. (Archive: I. Raming).

dience: Just do it! Become Catholic priests, reinterpret the ministry in the spirit of Jesus, and gather communities around you who may worship together with you... "(S. 51).

Looking back, I find Peter Rosien's statement forward-looking and correct, but not that of Norbert Scholl (and other authors who cast our ordination in a negative light at the time).

Reaction of the Vatican

Contrary to expectations, our action generated considerable attention in the Vatican. After all, if our ordination was invalid according to church law, it could be completely ignored!

Already on 10 July 2002, i.e. immediately after our ordination, the Congregation for the Doctrine of the Faith threatened us with excommunication. Its declaration was couched in unmistakable terms, announcing that we could only avert this severe punishment by "repentance" and "coming back into the fold". The Congregation for the Doctrine of the Faith could not cite any church law upon the basis of which the womenpriests could be excommunicated (as a so-called penalizable offence) by virtue of their actions. Nevertheless, the Congregation for the Doctrine of the Faith accused the seven women of having seriously violated "the divine constitution of the church" and of having acted contrary to the "definitive teachings of the church", which warranted "just punishment". Furthermore, the Congregation for the Doctrine of the Faith accused those involved in the ordination (both those administering and those receiving it) of simulating the Sacrament of Orders, thereby citing c. 1024 CIC ("Holy Orders are validly received by only a baptized man"). However, as is well known, simulation is to be understood as a conscious pretense, with there being a discrepancy between that which is outwardly stated and that which is inwardly desired. Our ordination was by no means a pretense, however. What was outwardly stated and the inner will were in complete agreement, both among those administering the Sacrament of Orders (the ordination) as well as those receiving it. Furthermore, c. 849, in contradiction to c. 1024, emphasizes that: "Baptism is the doorway to the sacraments".

- This also applies to the sacrament of priestly ordination. It is not the male gender that is the prerequisite for a valid ordination, but baptism in faith in Jesus Christ.

We women, however, were not brought off course either by threats from the Congregation for the Doctrine of the Faith or by their accusations. None of the seven women repented, nor did they recant. We publicly rejected the Vatican's accusations (for more information see www.virtuelle-dioezese.de), underscoring that the supposedly "definitive teachings of the church" were based on harsh discrimination of women – teachings which stand in stark contradiction to the biblical message ("in Christ" is "not male and female" on the basis of faith and baptism, Galatians 3:26) and therefore are not deserving of any recognition or attention. Thereupon the Congregation for the Doctrine of the Faith announced the excommunication of the seven women in January 2003.

The written correspondence with the Congregation for the Doctrine of the Faith is accessible to all interested parties and contains a testimony that is also of significance for the future of the church: It is documented therein that Catholic women refuse to bow to the discriminatory law excluding women from ordination (c. 1024 CIC) and that they are publicly standing up for their human dignity and human rights, including within the church.

The Vatican's drastic action could not prevent additional women's ordinations from being administered in various countries (Europe, the USA, Canada, etc.) in the following years. In response, the Congregation for the Doctrine of the Faith issued a general decree on 29 May 2008 on "The very serious crime of attempted ordination of a woman to the priesthood." It is stated in the decree that "anyone who administers the holy consecration to a woman, as well as any woman who seeks to receive the holy consecration, shall be subject to excommunication 'latae sententiae', which is reserved for the Apostolic See". The "offence of attempted ordination of women to the priesthood" is referred to as a "more serious offence" against the sacraments of the Church and is placed in the same category as the offence of sexual abuse of minors committed by clerics![4] The punishment of excommunication laid down in the decree is now also imposed on persons who publicly support the ordination of women, as the case of P. Roy Bourgeois has shown in an extreme way. If the ordination of women cements the "old clergy-based church" and strengthens its hierarchical structures, as some 'reform theologians' have claimed (see above on pp. 64f.), how does one explain the vehement opposition of the Church leadership to the ordination of women?

In contrast to these reform theologians, the representatives of the Church leadership in charge seem to be very well aware of the fundamental reforms of Church structures that would be set in motion by access of women to all ordained ministries. This is the only way to explain its massive resistance to the ordination of women, even against women being admitted to the diaconate!

When women overstep church law excluding them from the ordained ministries merely because of their gender (c. 1024), they are taking a very important step towards democratization of the hurch. For all women in the church, even those who do not aspire to the priesthood, this will logically enough lead to greater value

---

[4] Congregation for the Doctrine of the Faith (Normae de gravioribus delictis) of 19 December 2007, AAS 100(2008)403; see also Libreria Editrice Vaticana 2010.

being attached to their humanity; it creates an impulse towards a more dignified status for women – this is indeed a liberating development!

In the area of church offices, the hierarchy of the sexes is being overcome; by opening the ministries of deaconate and priesthood to women, the patriarchal nature of offices will be swept away, thereby triggering a reform of church structures. Reform of the hierarchical Roman system is prevented precisely by prohibition of the ordination of women. If the ordination of women really served the purpose of cementing this system, it would have to be warmly welcomed by the church leadership. Through the access of women to the diaconal and presbyteral ministry a freely chosen way of life will finally also replace the compulsory celibacy of priests – for men as well as for women in office.

See also this fundamental article:
I. Raming: Mutige Frauen stehen auf gegen ein ungerechtes Kirchengesetz – denn: "Ein ungerechtes Gesetz verpflichtet nicht" – "Lex iniusta non obligat" (published in "Imprimatur". Kritische Katholiken und ihre Zeitschrift, 2nd issue 2017, pp. 124–131)

The following poem, which we composed together soon after our ordination, provides some insight into our experiences and our thinking in the wake of our revolutionary step:

Womenpriests

We have crossed a threshold
We have crossed a barrier –
a barrier that says, "Women are not allowed to cross over!"
We opened a door that says, "No women allowed!"
We have leaped past the role assigned to women by men,
We have broken a law that holds women down.
…
Now we stand beyond the barrier, beyond the door, beyond the law …
We bear testament to this:
Women are called by God to be priests,
Women have been given the freedom of the 'children of God',
Women are allowed to raise their heads as free human beings,
Women are no longer enslaved by a law that suppresses women's vocations,
that destroys women's lives …
Voice from the Vatican (CDF):
Women have spoken out against the "divine constitution of the church".
They have meddled with the dominance of men over women.
They are encroaching upon the iron structures of the church – as desired by God,
    and instigated by Jesus,
preserved in tradition from the beginning.
They have acted against the "definitive teachings of the church".
They have "been a nuisance among the faithful". –

This is a "serious offence" that deserves the severest of punishments... !
Now the Patriarchs of the Hierarchy, the "vicars of God" are striking back.
They have realized how dangerous our actions are – if they are to retain their power.
They had not expected this from women – who have always meekly accepted everything. That is why we are being shunned by them – kicked out of their "*Communio*",
in which Jesus' love is betrayed.
We are being punished by them,
They seek to humiliate us before all the members of the church. They knock us to the ground – discarding us like refuse.
They say "you can't get away with this!"
We are the ones to show you the right way to "foster women", their "irreplaceable role", which only We know – the way to the "true dignity of women"!
They say: Women who let themselves be guided by Us shall be richly rewarded!
(and many accept this offer gratefully and gladly...)
You women who are still standing before the barrier, before the locked door –
Do you see, do you realize what's going on here?
Do you see how the power of the Hierarchy divides us? Divide et impera! – Divide and rule! –
When will you rise up against this arbitrariness? When will you seek the freedom of the 'children of God'?
When will you renounce the "spirit of bondage" and follow the "spirit of freedom" –
God's spiritual power, which moves wherever it wants – which everyone gives as he/she desires?

December 2002,
Ida Raming / Iris Müller
(published in: I. Raming: Roman Catholic Womenpriests, LIT-Verlag pp. 119f)

In the meantime, considerable scholarly work has been devoted to the actions of the Danube 7 in contravention of church law (c. 1024 CIC). This work has been summarized by *Barbara Velik-Frank* at the University of Graz and assessed as excellent:

Title: "Die Donaupriesterinnen – 'Danube Seven'. Eine heterotope Provokation" Publisher: tredition, Hamburg 2017 (A 2nd edition is in preparation)

In the restoration phase after the Council, several ***women's organisations*** were formed, which continue to work for the ordination of women:

- **1975**: Establishment of the "Women's Ordination Conference" (USA). This organization continues to work resolutely for the ordination of women to this day.
- **1987**: Founding of the "Mary of Magdala" – Initiative Gleichberechtigung für Frauen in der Kirche e.V. ("Initiative Equal Rights for Women in the Church") (due to lack of members, this organization does not exist at present)
- **1995**: Kirchen VolksBegehren starts up in Germany, after the platform 'We are Church' had already been founded in Austria in 1994. (Iris Müller, Ida Raming and many other reform-minded people were among the signatories).

The specific goals of *We are Church* include, in its own statements, a fraternal life in the Roman Catholic Church, a move away from *clericalism* while strengthening the community between laity and clergy as the *people of God*, the participation of all faithful stakeholders in decision-making processes in the Roman Catholic Church, *the equality of women* in the offices of the church. Additional demands include the abolition of obligatory *celibacy*, the proclamation of faith as *good news* and not as a "threat" as well as progress in *ecumenism*.

The second demand of the church petition *We are the Church*, which was signed by almost 2.5 million men and women in German-speaking countries alone in 1995, is:

Full equality for women

- Participation and co-decision-making in all church bodies
- Opening of the permanent diaconate to women
- Access of women to the priesthood (The exclusion of women from church offices cannot be justified on the basis of the Bible. The church can no longer forego the wealth of skills and life experiences offered by women. This also applies to administrative offices).

- **1996**: Foundation of the international organization "Women's Ordination Worldwide" (in Gmunden/Austria)

On the history of this organization (WOW)

In July 1996, nine members of the Women's Ordination Conference attended the first European Women's Synod in Gmunden, Austria. They went with hopes to forge an international strategy network to promote women's ordination in the Catholic Church. They were not disappointed.

At the outset, fourteen countries joined the budding international coalition, including Germany, Austria, Spain, Netherlands, the United Kingdom, Ireland, France, the United States, South Africa, Canada, Australia, New Zealand, Japan, and the Philippines. They named the network WOW — Women's Ordination Worldwide! Today, sixteen organizations from eleven different countries are represented.

The mission of Women's Ordination Worldwide:

> to promote worldwide the ordination of Roman Catholic women to a renewed priestly ministry in a democratic church, and to stand in solidarity with women who are ordained in the ongoing renewal of the church.

Although WOW is, at present, predominantly Roman Catholic, it does not exclude other religions working for the same aim, e.g., the Orthodox church and those Protestant traditions where women are not yet ordained. WOW held two international conferences, June 2001 in Dublin, Ireland and July 2005 in Ottawa, Canada. WOW is planning to hold the third international conference in 2010. This conference took place in 2015 in Philadelphia (USA).

IV   Developments under Pope Francis

Is this Pope open to reforms, also with regard to the position of women in the Church?

A promising statement made by this Pope appeared to offer a starting point or the foundations for a *volte-face*: e.g. Francis emphasized, for example (in his sermon from 12 May 2014):

"The Church does not have any office of door-closers... "Who are we to presume that we can close doors that the Holy Spirit wants to open? And, "It is the Holy Spirit who is bringing the Church... into the present today. We Christians should ask the Lord for the gift of obedience to the Holy Spirit... "

In terms of women and their status in the church, this would mean

Recognizing the spiritual callings of women to all ecclesial ministries, giving them dignity and allowing them to develop – for the urgently needed renewal of the church in the Spirit of Jesus Christ! – in accordance with the message delivered in the Letter to the Galatians (Galatians 3:26–28).

On several occasions, however, the Pope has publicly stated that he feels bound by the doctrinal decision of his predecessor (Pope John Paul II):

"The door to the ordination of women is closed... !"

For a critical view of this, see: Press statement by the international movement 'Roman Catholic Women Priests' (RCWP), German section:

The Pope's statements about the role of women in the church leave key questions unanswered

Since he assumed office, Pope Francis has spoken out several times on the role of women in the Catholic Church. In his last interview (in Sept. 2013), he argued that "the space for a dramatic female presence in the church must be widened". He added that women were indispensable for the church. The "female genius" is "necessary", he held, "in those places where important decisions are made", where "authority is exercised in the different areas of the church". The precondition for a more appropriate function of women in the church was in his view the elaboration of a "detailed theology of women", and deeper reflection on the "specific role and status of women".

While it is undoubtedly to be welcomed that the Pope is in favor of strengthening the presence and importance of women in the church, his statements nevertheless raise several serious questions: How can the participation of women in important ecclesial decisions, in the exercise of ecclesial authority, be achieved without granting women access to the offices of presbyterate and episcopate? On the other hand, the "door is closed" to access to these offices, according to the Pope's statement, with his reference to the "final" decision of his predecessor (John Paul II: *Ordinatio Sacerdotalis*, 1994). But as long as jurisdictional authority is bound to ordination and women are excluded from it, the Pope's statements about a strengthening of their role remain vague and non-committal. Nor is his reference to Mary's importance or to a theology of women" that is to be elucidated forward-looking. This is illustrated particularly clearly by negative experiences in the past with such a description of the "nature of women" drafted by men of the church!

A turning point towards full recognition of the personal dignity of women, their image in God and thus to their equal status and position in the church can only be achieved by a correct analysis of discrimination against women in the history of the church, which has yet to be performed down to the present day – after all, the exclusion of women from ordination and priestly office is clearly based on this discrimination against women, which has yet to be overcome!

God's holy spiritual power, which "he distributes to each one, just as she/he determines" (cf. 1 Corinthians 12:11), also calls women to the priestly ministry. This divine spiritual power is stronger than all the obstacles that a patriarchally skewed and deformed theology puts in its way.

In the growing *international movement of Roman Catholic Women Priests* (RCWP), women can already now actively place their priestly vocation at the service of people. This thus performs an important pioneering function in the entire Catholic Church by creating a tradition conducive to women in the Roman Catholic Church, which continues to be dominated by patriarchal structures.

For the international movement of 'Roman Catholic Women Priests' (RCWP), German section: Ida Raming, Dr. theol., Stuttgart (Germany), September 2013 (published in: Römisch-katholische Priesterinnen. Lit-Verlag 2013, pp. 124f)

Press release: Women's Ordination Conference (USA) from November 2016:

Clear criticism was directed at the repeated rejection of ordination of women by Pope Francis, who makes reference to the "final prohibition" (*Ordinatio Sacerdotalis*, 1994) issued by John Paul II:

Patriarchy Will Not Have the Last Word

For immediate release: 1 November 2016. Contact: Kate McElwee

On the papal plane from Sweden to Rome, Pope Francis was asked by a journalist:

- **"Is it realistic to think that there might be women priests in the next few decades?"**
- On the Ordination of women in the Catholic church, the last word is clear," Francis responded, before mentioning John Paul's 1994 apostolic letter banning the practice, *Ordinatio Sacerdotalis*. "It was given by St. John Paul II and this remains."
- **"But really forever? Never?"**
- "If we read carefully the declaration made by St. John Paul II it goes in that direction."

The Women's Ordination Conference (WOC) is profoundly disappointed with Pope Francis's reliance on his predecessors' documents regarding the possibility of priestly ordination for women.

Several times Pope Francis has been asked by journalists aboard the papal plane regarding women's priestly ordination. The reason this question cannot be suppressed is because the exclusion of women defies the example of Jesus, who welcomed men and women equally.

Ordinatio Sacerdotalis is an outdated, fallible and painful document created by his predecessors to diminish the leadership and vocations of women.

Instead of citing John Paul II, Pope Francis might have cited the Vatican's own *Pontifical Biblical Commission* that concluded in 1976 that there is no valid scriptural or theological reason for denying ordination to women, or looked to archeology and historical documents that show women's leadership in the early Church. He could have looked to Jesus who welcomed women as his equal. Or he could look to the people of God who overwhelmingly support the ordination of women.

The Church cannot be afraid to examine customs when they no longer communicate or resonate with the Gospel. A Church that is not open to the gifts of half of its membership is unsustainable and out of touch with the needs of its people. "Never changing" is not only historically inaccurate but simply not an option when it comes to women's equality.

The Women's Ordination Conference and the majority of U.S. Catholics we represent do not accept "never ever" as an option. We will continue to work for the full equality of women in the Roman Catholic Church, knowing that unjust laws are indefensible with a God that does not discriminate. Patriarchy will not have the last word.

"In Christ there is no Jew or Greek, slave or citizen, male or female. All are one in Christ Jesus." – Galatians 3:28

"Humankind was created as God's reflection: in the divine image God created them, female and male, God made them." – Genesis 1:27

©2018 Women's Ordination Conference PO Box 15057, Washington, DC 20003 (202) 675–1006 (Seite 83–85)

V Prospects

Our aim and objective is: complete equality for women in all services and offices of the Church, which has yet to be achieved.

When will this goal, this vision, finally become reality?

We are witnessing a Pope (Francis) for whom, although he is committed to reforms in the church, the question of women is not one of his priority topics.

We must rationally acknowledge this.

His "theology of women" – his vision of the church ("she is a woman!") – while paradoxically it is represented only by men in office!) as well as his conception of Mariology are hyperbolic:

"Mary towers high above the bishops ... !"

This raises the question: What specific (including legal) consequences has this had for women in the Church? So far none!

"Gaudete et Exsultate" – Rejoice and exult!

This is the title of the new Apostolic Letter of Pope Francis (2018).

In it, the Pope rightly emphasizes the calling of every Christian to achieve holiness: *"We are all called upon to be holy, to live in love and offer our personal witness in daily action, each in the place where he/she is"* (no. 14). In his letter, the Pope also expresses his recognition of important female saints: *"With regard to these different paths (to holiness) I would like to emphasize that the 'female genius' is also manifested in female paths to holiness, which are indispensable in reflecting the holiness of God in this world... .* In this context, he mentions the names of well-known female saints: *Hildegard of Bingen, Bridget of Sweden, Catherine of Siena, Teresa of Avila and Thérèse of Lisieux*, and praises their significance in important reforms in the church (no. 12).

But it is precisely in these statements that we are once again directly confronted with the clichéd, narrow view of the "nature of women", which Pope Francis, as is well known, has often expressed. For what does his characterization of *"female paths to holiness"* have to do with the message of the Gospel? No distinction is made here between male and female (cf. Galatians 3:26–28: "For in Christ Jesus *you are all sons and daughters of God by faith. For all of you who were baptized into Christ, you have clothed yourself with Christ... There is nei-*

ther... *male and female, for you are all one in Christ Jesus.*") The grand goal of holiness worth seeking can be achieved by anyone only through courage, bravery, trust in God, strength of soul, love of one's neighbor – with God's help. What does this have to do with being *male* or *female*?

The gender stereotype propagated by the Pope with its consequences for the position of women in the church has a deleterious effect on them with fatal consequences: Women are prevented from developing their personality; they are emasculated as individuals. This too is an essential constraint on their calling to sainthood. In the Roman Catholic Church, they are denied the possibility to develop their calling to the priesthood. (*St. Theresa of Lisieux* is a tragic example of this!)

The flip side of these repeated praises attesting to the "female genius" is the persistent and ongoing oppression of women in the church. It casts a gloomy shadow on the reform efforts of this Pope, which otherwise deserve acknowledgement.

As a reminder: Pope John Paul II coined the expression "female genius" in his Apostolic Letter "*Mulieris Dignitatem*" (1988), but at the same time he underscores in it the alleged gender-based exclusion of women from the priesthood. He refers in this context to "the *God-given relationship between man and woman, between the »feminine« and the »masculine«, both in the mystery of creation and in the mystery of redemption" (no. 50)*. This was soon followed, in 1994, by the "definitive" prohibition of the ordination of women in his letter *Ordinatio Sacerdotalis*, which Pope Francis still declares to be binding today.

The praises of women voiced by the popes (and theologians) must therefore be regarded with great suspicion. They prove to be deceiving and spurious as long as women are denied equal rights and thus denied full membership in the church.

Jamie Manson, theologian and author, warns in her article *(NCR from 13 April 2018)* as follows:
"*Should women rejoice over 'Gaudete et Exsultate'?,*
 pointedly noting:
"It's time to be honest about Pope Francis and women"
 and asks crucial questions:
"Can women really achieve wholeness in an institutional church that does not see them as equal? Can women grow into holiness under a pope who insists that they are incapable of administering sacred rites? Can women reach the fullness of life to which God calls them in a church that rejects their gifts and bars them from ministering to the body of Christ? As long as these limits remain on a woman's ability to be fully alive in her church, there will be serious limits on the extent to which she can truly rejoice and be glad."

The late Protestant theologian **Marga Bührig**, who as feminist theologian fought for complete equality of women, posed a crucial question (in 1987), which we can also pass on to Pope Francis: *"If women can be saints, why can't they also be priests?"*

Indeed, the fact of the matter is: if and when women can be saints, even more so can they be priests!

The Roman Catholic Church urgently needs such holy women-priests (presbyteresses) and bishops!

Ida Raming (May 2018)

Pope Francis feels bound by the theologically untenable doctrinal documents of his predecessors regarding the ordination of women. Is this because of a fear to advocate and work for progress in this field?

Unfortunately, there are many bishops gathered in the Vatican/Curia who vehemently oppose any and all needed reforms, which means that the Pope must live among enemies, among "wolves". This has been amply demonstrated by experience of the past, and the small reform steps taken by the Pope have clearly illustrated this.

Nevertheless, the movement for the liberation of women must and will carry on. It is produced by the working of the Holy Spirit, "who will guide you into all the truth" (John 16:13).

In Catholic women's associations, impatience is mounting in view of the refusal to institute reforms.

• Prophetic, energetic steps are necessary!

One of these forward-looking steps is our "womenpriests movement", which was initiated in 2002. In the meantime, this movement has spread internationally (to several continents and countries). *Dr. Patricia Fresen* (priest and bishop), born in South Africa, English-speaking, has made a significant contribution to this movement through her work (travels to various countries); (membership numbered 250 as of March 2018, and now, in 2020: approximately 300; several candidates are preparing for their ordination). In several countries, women with a calling are already performing priestly ministries, thus promoting the gifts of women, including their self-confidence.

Elsie Hainz McGrath, Bridget M. Meehan, Ida Raming (eds.): Frauen finden einen Weg: Die internationale Bewegung Römisch-katholische Priesterinnen, LIT Verlag, 2009. (English title: "Women find a Way: the movement and stories of Roman Catholic Womenpriests").

On the development of the Roman Catholic Womenpriests movement (RCWP):

Women should increasingly realize that they cannot be expected to obey a profoundly unjust law (c. 1024 CIC) that discriminates against women (*lex iniusta non obligat!* This is an old, recognized principle of law!).

The "**question of power**" is cropping up as a problem in discussions ever more often: Men of the church do not want to share with women the power that is associated with ministries and service. This is a major obstacle for women in the church!

This attitude is disgraceful, and it is not guided by the Christian spirit: "Not so with you ... ! (Mathew 20, 25f)

On this, see the following **literature**:

- **Irmtraud Fischer, Christoph Heil (eds.):**
  Geschlechterverhältnisse und Macht. Lebensformen in der Zeit des frühen Christentums, vol. 21, LIT Verlag 2010;

- **Monika Egger, Livia Meier et al. (eds.)**
  WoMan in Church. Kirche und Amt im Kontext der Geschlechterfrage, vol. 20, 2006 (LIT-Verlag)
- **Helen Schüngel-Straumann**
  Die Frau am Anfang. Eva und die Folgen, 2nd edition, LIT Verlag, Münster 1997

- The question involving the **relationship between state and church** taking into account the aspect of the women's question opens an important problem area as well as new strategies: Can democratic states tolerate discrimination based on gender (as in the Roman Catholic Church) under the rubric of "religious freedom"? Should they have not intervened and taken action against this long ago in order to remain true to their constitution? What is the value of the oath of allegiance to our constitution which is taken by bishops in Germany before they assume office?

On this, see:
Stella Ahlers: Gleichstellung der Frau in Staat und Kirche – ein problematisches Spannungsverhältnis,
Series: ReligionsRecht im Dialog, vol. 2, 2005, LIT Verlag.
In addition:
Denise Buser: Die unheilige Diskriminierung. Eine juristische Auslegeordnung für die Interessensabwägung zwischen Geschlechtergleichstellung u. Religionsfreiheit beim Zugang zu religiösen Leitungsämtern. Series: Religionsrecht im Dialog, vol. 16, 2014, LIT Verlag.
op cit.: Unholy Discrimination… Series: Religionsrecht im Dialog, vol. 25, 2017, LIT Verlag.
On this topic, see also the following activist letter by *Maria Hollering-Hamers*:

To the Federal Ministry of Justice   Lichtenfels, 10 February 2017
Federal Minister of Justice Maas
Mohrenstraße 37
11015 Berlin

Dear Minister Maas,

I suppose I am not the first woman to approach you regarding the problem of the lack of gender equality, and I am sure I will not be the last. However, I am so moved by this problem that I would like to use this letter to try once again to make my request heard by you. I am concerned about the discrimination and exclusion of women in the Roman Catholic Church.

Since our Constitution, the Basic Law, states in Article 3 that discrimination on the basis of gender is prohibited and adds very hopefully in the second paragraph that the state will promote actual implementation of equal rights for women and men and work towards the elimination of existing disadvantages, I cannot understand why so many Roman Catholic women have to accept men who lead the church discriminating against them.

I know that the Act on Freedom of Religion states that churches are free to organize and administer their affairs independently within the limits of law applicable to everyone. It would still be acceptable for churches to be allowed to assign persons to their offices without the involvement of the state if they had to comply with Article 3 of the Constitution when doing so, and if no church could discriminate against people on the basis of gender when awarding offices, which is quite normal and completely accepted when posting job vacancies in the non-religious world of work.

I am of the opinion that these limits, which apply to everyone, are clearly overstepped here and that lawmakers pervert this article to such an extent that church leaders are simply legally allowed to discriminate against women. I am outraged by this travesty... and I am not the only one!

Freedom of religion, a precious right in our country, can in my opinion also be realized without discrimination against women. Surely it cannot be that this must always remain so because men have managed, in the course of two thousand years of history, to garner leading offices and functions for themselves by successfully preventing women from developing and educating themselves. Social conditions have changed, the status of women has changed and the church refuses to draw the right conclusions regarding these changes and share power to create just structures.

Then the state should help out! Should not Article 3 of the Basic Law, this important article for which the "Mothers of the Basic Law" fought so hard, be placed in the hierarchy above Article 4 laying down religious freedom? Freedom of religion means first and foremost that everyone has the freedom to choose his or her own religion and to decide to practice one's religion freely and without restrictions. One can do both without one-half of the people who are members of a religion excluding or discriminating against the other half of its members. Is this always supposed to remain like this? Should the daughters, the generation of daughters-in-law and granddaughters always and forever be victims of this injustice, fighting futile battles because lawmakers are afraid to take on that colossus of power, the Catholic Church, and to place these richly ornate men within the limits of the Basic Law?

As Catholic women, we are not only part of the church, but also part of the state, and we can expect and demand that our right to equal treatment, including within the church, be safeguarded.

I ask you to take up this grave injustice and change the law on religious freedom so that it also applies within a religious community: women and men are equal! Keep your promise laid down in section 2 and work towards the elimination of the disadvantages that Catholic women face!

A subject very closely related to this is the payment of bishops and archbishops by the state. Men are highly paid with taxpayers' money from men and women, even though it is a profession that without exception women are not allowed to take up. This as well would appear to me to be in flagrant contradiction to our Constitution, the Basic Law. In the "normal" life of citizens it has long been accepted that jobs must be equally accessible to women and men. Why don't you in your capacity as lawmaker take action here? The principle of equal treatment has been massively violated here for over two centuries.

I hope you will not answer me with a vacuous letter that will not do anything to change the status quo! I already have such letters and similar in my desk drawer. I want justice for women, including in the church, because our Basic Law guarantees it.

With best regards:

Maria Hollering-Hamers

(This letter, which unfortunately remained unanswered, is published on the website of the Kirchen-VolksBewegung – Diözesangruppe Eichstätt).

So the search for truth, rights and justice – to finally also be granted to women in the Roman Catholic Church – will continue and will lead to the goal – by the grace of God and the Holy Spirit!

• In the following: Some (small) signs of hope from the recent past: More and more people in the Church are publicly speaking out in favor of women's ordination:

"The ban on ordination is antiquated"

Swiss clerics are reviving the discussion on the ordination of women. This is a good thing: local womenpriests are of more use to congregations than clergymen flown in from India. Simon Hehli 28 February 2018: (Article from the NZZ, 28 February 2018):

Abbot Martin Werlen promotes the ordination of women
(Alessandro della Valle/Keystone)

Getting right to the point is often not a strength of theologians. Many of them tend to use long, convoluted sentences. In certain passages this also applies to Martin Werlen's new book "Zu spät" ("Too Late"), which is soaring towards the top of the bestseller list. But one statement by the former abbot of Einsiedeln stands out crystal clear: "The more time passes, the more convinced I am that the exclusion of women from the ordained priesthood is one of those traditions that can and must be changed." It should be noted that this statement comes from a cleric who a few years ago was accused by the media of refusing to take a clear position in favor of the ordination of women to the priesthood. Well, it is a good thing that he finally has.

The topic of women's ordination has preoccupied progressive believers for decades, without much hope for change having developed to date. In the meantime, the Bishop of Basel, Felix Gmür, has also signaled that this "does not have to go on forever". Traditionalists, on the other hand, insist that the priest must be male, since he acts "in persona Christi" at Holy Mass. And Pope Francis is fobbing off Catholics with the supposedly so important "Marian dimension" of the

Church. Such arguments can only be perceived as antiquated and discriminatory in Western society. Women should not be able to be priests? The *Christkatholiken*, a regional German Catholic church, serves as evidence that it is very possible indeed. The German theologian Karl Rahner also stated long ago that there is no coherent ecclesiastical or historical argument to exclude women from the ordained ministry.

8 February 2018, 10:07 (commentary)

Of course, the ordination of women would not solve all the problems of the Catholic Church. The Reformed Church has had female pastors for a long time, and this has not prevented the decline of the institution in the course of secularization. But the admission of womenpriests would be one tried and tested means to slow down the further alienation of women from the Catholic Church – and often it remains merely the women faithful and lay theologians who keep Church life going. In times marked by an acute lack of priests, such a step would also be more attractive than the merging of parishes or the recruitment of priests from India and Africa, who have difficulties with local customs and language.

Nothing can be expected from the "reform Pope" Francis with regard to the ordination of women. The Argentinean has made it clear several times that he is not ready to alter the final "no" from his predecessor John Paul II. The last word in this matter has been clearly spoken. According to this logic, reforms that disregard what any Pope has stated at any given time would be impossible for all times. Nevertheless, Catholics in Switzerland should not be overly impressed by Vatican proclamations and should continue their discussion about womenpriests with vigor – just like the debate over abolition of compulsory celibacy, which is no longer in tune with the times.

The Vatican will one day realize that the same rigid rules cannot apply worldwide: What may be right for booming congregations in Black Africa may prove to be the death knell for the People's Church in Western Europe. It would be a good topic of conversation when Francis comes to Switzerland in June. But the bishops there will hardly be able to muster up the courage to broach this issue.

Martin Werlen rekindles the discussion on priestly ordination for women

Martin Werlen likes to provoke people: The former abbot of Einsiedeln believes that it is high time the Catholic Church allowed women to become priests.

"God has called upon me"

As a teenager, her friends prophesied to her that she would one day become pope. This is not going to happen – but Jacqueline Straub firmly believes that in 20 years

she will be a Catholic woman-priest. (Simon Hehli, Lucerne 9 June 2015, 10:00 a.m.).

Jacqueline Straub is one of the brave pioneers who has fought for women's ordination in Switzerland. She preaches in open-minded congregations and has published several books on the subject:

"Jung, katholisch, weiblich – Weshalb ich Priesterin werden will" – Jacqueline Straub
Available from Publik Forum Verlag.
 "Endlich Priesterin sein" – Jacqueline Straub
Available from Paulus Verlag
 "Young, Catholic, Female." – Jacqueline Straub
Available from Fisher King Publishing.

- From the **Ecumenical Congress in Osnabrück** (Dec. 2017) on this topic "Women in Church Offices" has radiated signs of hope. As a participant in this important event, I described the positive impression it created in an article:

Oekumenischer Kongress zum Thema "Frauen in kirchlichen Ämtern" setzt neue Maßstäbe
Ida Raming

"It is not the access of women to church services and offices that needs to be justified, but their exclusion" -

This is one of the 7 basic theses that were formulated at the Ecumenical Congress in Osnabrück held in December 2017, which was approved by a majority of the participants. Another thesis (no. 1) is:

"The declared goal of the ecumenical movement, the visible unity of the churches, cannot be achieved without an agreement on the presence of women in all church offices".

It was a significant event, especially since this Congress was the first one held in ecumenical cooperation, with the participation of the Universities of Osnabrück, Münster and Oldenburg and women's associations from both Christian

Churches, Catholic and Lutheran. About 200 people took part in this forward-looking meeting. Numerous persons: Female theologians and some male theologians, officeholders from both churches spoke, exploring the overall situation of the Church regarding women in church offices from different perspectives (biblical, dogmatic, church history, sociological).

Reports from both the Lutheran and the Catholic Church testified, with impressive examples, that "on the question of women's access to church services and ministries... many wounds have been caused in all Christian traditions" – wounds which "still hurt today". The most recent example is Latvia, where the ordination of women in the Protestant Church has been reversed!

With reference to the Apostolic Letter of Pope John Paul II: *Ordinatio Sacerdotalis* (1994), it was stressed that "to this day"... "fears of impending sanctions 'accompany' the topic of ordination of women! Nevertheless, several speakers did not shy away from challenging and rejecting this allegedly "final" letter (OS). This included from the canonical side (Prof. S. Demel) on the basis of several canons from the CIC, with Prof. S. Wendel rejecting in drastic terms an "argumentation" constantly repeated – not least by several bishops: *"Jesus was a man – and only men can therefore represent him in the ordained ministry"*. She showed that such a manner of speaking is based on a very primitive, static conception of the human gender, which moreover ignores the fundamental truth that biological "gender" has no meaning (in the sense of a value standard) in the area of religion.

Dr. Franz Josef Bode (Diocese of Osnabrück) was the only bishop present at the conference. He listened to the lectures and engaged in discussion. He is the head of the Pastoral Commission in the German Bishops' Conference and also chairs the sub-commission 'Women in Church and Society'. He emphasized that: "The church must analyze and evaluate the results of the congress." He stated that he was going to introduce the question of women's access to church offices and services in the Bishops' Conference in the form of a working group. The Roman Congregation for the Doctrine of the Faith, he stated, could certainly address it.

In this undertaking he is likely to encounter strong resistance, for all too many bishops do not want to meddle with the present structure, which assigns them lofty supremacy – they reject women with primitive arguments, without regard to the bequest of Jesus:

"It shall not be so with you... !" (Mathew 20:25–28) and to take into account the results of historical-critical Bible exegesis in general.

One "red thread" running through many presentations was the message setting out fundamental principles in the letter by the Apostle Paul to the Galatian Church:

"So in Christ Jesus you are all sons and daughters of God through faith. For since you were baptized into Christ, you have clothed yourself with Christ. There is no longer 'Jew

or Gentile, no longer 'slave or free', no longer 'male and female', for you are all one in Christ Jesus" (Galatians 3:26–28).

As is well known, this promise has yet to be realized in the structures of the Roman Catholic Church! – The memory of the great disciple **Mary of Magdala,** *'Apostola Apostolorum',* was also very present in presentations and speeches at the Congress. Her testimony of the risen Christ will endure – against the anti-spirit of patriarchal retention of power and oppression of women.

With regard to the situation of the Roman Catholic Church, marked by the continuing refusal to take needed reform steps, the "prophetic" words of *Michael Gorbachev* were recalled: *"He who comes too late will be punished by life!"*

Representatives of Catholic women's associations (KDFB and Kfd) therefore expressly abandoned their previous unilateral commitment to the demand for a female deaconate. Instead, they demanded access of women to all church services and ministries; for the participants in the congress it was discernible: the patience of women has long since been worn thin.

Some participants therefore spoke out emphatically for "clear symbols of resistance", for "militant, prophetic steps" on the way to final recognition of the personal dignity of women in the Catholic Church. In the same vein, the action taken by the 7 'Danube priestesses' against unjust canon law excluding women from ordination (c. 1024 CIC) was expressly acknowledged. (published in the magazine "Imprimatur", vol. 1, 2018, pp. 23–25)

What was new about this event, in my view, was that the Catholic women's associations distanced themselves from the narrow focus on the diaconate of women, demanding the opening of all offices to women. In addition, the participants were encouraged by Dr. Claudia Lücking-Michel (a member of the ZDK) in particular to take a clear, courageous and tough stand on women's ordination.

Ecumenical Congress, 6–9 December 2017 in Osnabrück
WOMEN IN ECCLESIASTICAL OFFICES
Reform movements in ecumenism

OSNABRÜCK THESES

From 6 to 9 December 2017, a scholarly congress involving ecumenical collaboration between institutions for theology at the universities of Osnabrück, Oldenburg and Münster as well as Roman Catholic and Protestant associations and institutions took place in Osnabrück to address the topic "Women in Church Offices. Reform movements in ecumenism". With the majority of votes from more than 120 participating individuals from the areas of multilateral ecumenism and from

Germany and abroad, the following theses were adopted following lectures, talks and intensive consultations:

1. The declared goal of the ecumenical movement, the visible unity of the churches, cannot be achieved without an agreement on the presence of women in all church offices.
2. Women in church offices profoundly change the view of each community of faith, both of itself and of others.
3. It is not the access of women to church services and ministries that must be justified, but their exclusion.
4. The discussion about whether God has given an unalterable instruction as to how or by whom God is to be witnessed through church office can and must remain open-ended.
5. The distinction between specific services within one (sacramental) ministry (episcopate, presbyterate and diaconate) has evolved historically and can be further developed with an ecumenical perspective. All forms of service should be opened to women. Care must be taken to ensure that no gender-specific definitions are laid down.
6. Critical questions regarding the development of church doctrine with regard to the exclusion of women from church services and ministries are evidence of the willingness of women to exercise their calling to serve in the proclamation of the gospel in word and deed.
7. The Spirit of Jesus Christ obligates us to always deal with the different theological convictions regarding the question of church offices with appreciation while reconciling arguments in our interactions with one another.

VOWS

1. In the assumption and exercise of church office, we shall make gender justice the touchstone of credibility in the proclamation of the gospel. This is indispensable in the apostolic mission of the Churches. Beyond the question of the ordination of women, other forms in which gender justice is shaped and developed in an overly insensitive manner in the Churches are also to be identified and overcome.
2. We shall continue theological discussions regarding the presence of women in all church offices with the aim of reaching an understanding in the remaining disputes. We shall not – depending on the confessional situation – sidestep or avoid critical discussion with the responsible church leaders about all forms of ordained ministry. In ecumenical fellowship, we are committed to the ordination of women to the positions of deaconesses, presbyters (pastors, priests) and bishops.

3. We will continue to make theological contributions to the needed differentiation between the opening of the diaconate and other ministries to women within the one (sacramental) ordo. The diaconate as a ministry for men and women reinforces the basic diaconal orientation of the church.
4. We shall work for an increasing participation of women in leadership positions and ministries in our area of responsibility. We shall strive for a culture of partnership in all churches.

Osnabrück, 9 December 2017
Prof. Dr. Margit Eckholt, University of Osnabrück
Prof. Dr Ulrike Link-Wieczorek, University of Oldenburg
Prof. Dr Dorothea Sattler, University of Münster
Prof. Dr. Andrea Strübind, University of Oldenburg

- A brave, committed group: "Aktionskreis Kirchenreform Ingolstadt" has been publicly campaigning for decades for women's access to all offices in the church. It frequently holds vigils at important church events, including most recently (March 2018).

Annelie and Walter Hürter are long-standing inspirers and sponsors of this action group. Their trenchant banner: **Stop excluding women!**

How do you see the chances for the admission of women in ordained ministries of the Catholic Church?

Response by W. Hürter:

"I believe that the skills of women are increasingly being recognized in politics and society. The exclusively male-dominated church must realize that it cannot ignore this fact.

This is not a core question of faith, nor is it about lagging behind the Zeitgeist, but about acting in tune with the times according to the principle "ecclesia semper reformanda est" (a church which must always renew itself), in other words, the church is always in need of reform!
from: *Donaukurier* from 15 March 2018

Annelie Hürter has documented the ongoing reform process with some fitting illustrations. Here are a few examples:

- In her book "Der Weiberaufstand. Warum Frauen in der katholischen Kirche mehr Macht brauchen" (Kösel-Verlag Munich 2017) the journalist **Dr. Christiane Florin** shows with drastic examples that Catholic women are all too conformist and (so far) have not dared to rise up in rebellion as is needed: *"Very few want to fight, although they opt for confrontational vocabulary in private discussions: Discrimination, derision, contempt. Anyone who asks women in the Church about women registers a blend of hard words with soft behavior. Those who are discriminated against, belittled, and disregarded display consideration, caution and leniency towards the institution and its representatives"* (164). The author is not satisfied with this behavior. As she explains: *"The women's uprising means not only asking, but demanding. The women's uprising is about a power struggle. Women like to keep silent about this"* (pg. 171)

This book has clearly stimulated a change in direction in the docile conformist behavior not only characterizing Catholic women's associations. But will this positive effect be a lasting one?

- On International Women's Day (8 March 2018), some courageous women spoke out in Rome:

Former Irish President *Mary McAleese* expressed frustration with the way the Catholic hierarchy treats women in the church. She said at a congress held in Rome that concrete steps towards more power for women still needed to be taken.

While she was hopeful at the beginning of Pope Francis' term of office, she is now very disappointed, said *McAleese*. Although the "genius" and "mystery" of women is being invoked, concrete steps towards greater participation of women in church leadership are lacking, McAleese remarked Wednesday at the opening of the congress in Rome...

McAleese was speaking at the event presenting a conference on the presence and status of women in the Catholic Church. The meeting, taking place on the occasion of International Women's Day on Thursday, is being organized by the platform "Voices of Faith"...

McAleese called **the exclusion of women from ordination "misogyny disguised as theology**"...

- The Tübingen theologian **Johanna Rahner** has called for greater appreciation and more co-determination for women in the Catholic Church. "The church will continue to lose credibility if we do not achieve equal rights for men and women," said Rahner on Friday evening at a ceremony marking the 50th anniversary of the Diocesan Council in the Archdiocese of Freiburg. It is high time to dare more gender justice and more democracy... (catholic.de from 17 March 2018)
- In the interesting article "Priests are dying out" ("Stimmen der Zeit", May 2018) **Stefan Kiechle SJ** strongly advocates the ordination of women in view of declining numbers of priests: "Why not seize the opportunity to finally consecrate women? Since John Paul II, this idea has been subject to a gag order on thought and speech – but can this be seriously enforced or is it even desirable for it to be enforced in times of crisis and at the same time enlightenment? Especially since feminist theology and the women's movement have offered new insights, since then there is no turning back?... "
- As a sign of hope, Pope Francis' energetic appeal to young people before the Synod of Youth 2018 is worth citing: *"Be courageous, state openly what you want! Make a fuss... !*

In the final document issued by the **preparatory meeting of the Synod of Bishops** (in October 2018) on the topic "Young people, faith and different vocations", young people expressed their aspirations for reform of the Church: "*This document is intended for the Synod Fathers. It is to serve as a compass for the bishops to better understand young people... The Church can play a crucial role in ensuring that these young people are not marginalized, but feel accepted. This can happen if we try to strengthen the dignity of women – within the church and also in other social contexts.* **Even today there is a general social problem that women are still not afforded equal status (as men). The same applies to the church..."**

The **BDKJ** (Bund deutscher katholischer Jugend) has spoken out more energetically for Church reforms regarding the status of women in the church: The BDKJ supports the proposal by the Pontifical Commission for Latin America to convene a synod of bishops on the topic of women: "*The BDKJ is pleased about this initiative*". In her statement, Federal President Lisi Maier underscores that: **"Our Church, however, cannot credibly demand equal rights for girls and women in society if it denies women the same rights as men within its own structures."** Therefore the synod must also "address 'hot topics' and discuss the admission of women to the ordained ministries..." (katholisch.de from 18 April 2018).

(Is it taken into consideration, however, that in a synod of bishops only bishops, i.e. solely men, have decision-making power, in this case over women? Structurally, this is not only antiquated, but also deeply unfair and discriminating towards women – they are still subject to male domination!)

- Immediately before the completion of this documentation, I received news from the Vatican that the **Prefect of the Congregation for the Doctrine of the Faith, Luis F. Ladaria** S.J., in an article of the *Osservatore Romano* on 29 June 2018, had reaffirmed the "no" to the ordination of women to the priesthood. The allegedly definitive ban on the ordination of women to the priesthood was first pronounced in the Apostolic Letter *Ordinatio Sacerdotalis* (1994) by Pope John Paul II.

Below is the text of the article:

Regarding some doubts as to the definitive nature of the doctrine of *Ordinatio sacerdotalis*
29 May 2018

"Stay in me and I'll stay in you. Just as a branch cannot bear fruit of itself, but only if it remains on the vine, so you too, if you do not remain in me" (John 15:4). It is only thanks to its rootedness in Jesus Christ, its founder, that the Church can bring life and salvation to the whole world. This rooting is primarily through the sacraments, at the center of which is the Eucharist. Instituted by Christ, the sacraments are the foundation of the Church, which it continually builds as His body and bride. Deeply connected with the Eucharist is the Sacrament of Orders, through which Christ makes himself present to the church as the source of its life and action. Priests are made "in Christ's image" "so that they may act *in persona Christi Capitis*" (*Presbyterorum ordinis*, n. 2).

Christ wanted to bestow this sacrament on the twelve apostles, who were all men, and they in turn entrusted other men with it. The Church has always been bound by this decision of the Lord, which excludes valid bestowal of the priesthood of ministry on women. John Paul II stated in the Apostolic Letter *Ordinatio sacerdotalis* from 22 May 1994: "Therefore, in order to remove all doubt concerning the important matter concerning the divine constitution of the Church herself, I declare by virtue of my ministry of strengthening the brethren (cf. Luke 22:32) that the church has no authority to ordain female priests and that all the faithful of the church must definitively abide by this decision" (n. 4). The Congregation for the Doctrine of the Faith, in response to a question raised on the doctrine of *Ordinatio sacerdotalis*, affirmed that this is a truth that belongs to the church's *depositum fidei*.

In this light, I am greatly concerned that in some countries voices can be heard which are once again casting doubt on the definitive nature of the teachings mentioned. To argue that this doctrine is not definitive, it is held that it has not been defined *ex cathedra* and could therefore be modified by a future pope or council. The spreading of such doubts arouses great confusion among the faithful, not only with regard to the sacrament of Orders, which is part of the divine constitution of the church, but also with regard to the ordinary Magisterium, which can lay down Catholic doctrine infallibly.

Concerning the first point: As far as the priesthood of ministry is concerned, the church knows that the impossibility of female ordination is part of the "substance" of the sacrament (cf. DH 1728). The church does not have the power to change this substance, because it is through the sacraments instituted by Christ that it is built as a church. It is not only a question of discipline, but of doctrine, because it concerns the structure of the sacraments, the original places of encounter with Christ and the transmission of faith. We are not therefore faced with a constraint that would prevent the church from fulfilling her mission in the world more effectively. If the church cannot intervene in this question, the reason is that the original love of God intervenes here. He himself acts in the ordination of priests, so that in the church, always and in every situation of its history, Jesus Christ is visible and effective "as the principal source of grace" (Pope Francis, *Evangelii gaudium*, n. 104).

In the awareness that it cannot change this tradition out of obedience to the Lord, this is also why the church strives to deepen its meaning. For the will of Jesus Christ, the Logos, is never without meaning. The priest acts in the person of Christ, the Bridegroom of the Church, and his being a man is an indispensable aspect of this sacramental representation (cf. Congregation for the Doctrine of the Faith, *Inter insigniores*, no. 5).

Certainly, the differences in the tasks performed by men and women does not imply subordination, but rather mutual enrichment. It should be remembered that the perfect image of the church is Mary, the Mother of the Lord, to whom the apostolic ministry has not been entrusted. In this way it becomes evident that the original language of being man and woman, which the Creator inscribed in the human body, has been absorbed in the work of our redemption. It is precisely fidelity to Christ's plan with the priesthood of ministry, therefore, that allows the specific role of women in the church to become ever more profound and promoted, because "in the Lord there is neither woman without man nor man without woman" (1 Corinthians 11:11). In this way a light can also shine on our culture, which has difficulty in understanding the meaning and beauty of the difference between men and women, which also relates to their complementary mission in society.

Regarding the second point, doubts raised about the definitive character of *Ordinatio sacerdotalis* also have serious implications for the way of understanding the Magisterium of the church. It is important to affirm that infallibility refers not only to solemn declarations made by a Council or to papal definitions *ex cathedra*, but also to the ordinary and universal Magisterium of Bishops scattered throughout the world when they, in communion with one another and with the Pope, present Catholic doctrine as definitively binding. John Paul II referred to this infallibility in *Ordinatio sacerdotalis*. He did not, therefore, proclaim a new dogma, but rather, in order to remove any doubt, with the authority conferred on him as the Successor of Peter, reaffirmed in a formal declaration what the ordinary and universal Magisterium has proclaimed throughout history as belonging to the good of the faith. It is precisely this way of exposition that corresponds to a style of ecclesial communion, because the Pope did not want to act alone, but as a witness in listening to an uninterrupted and living tradition. Moreover, no one will deny that the Magisterium can infallibly comment on truths that are necessarily linked to the formally revealed good. For only in this way can it fulfil its task of preserving and faithfully interpreting the goods of faith in a holy way.

Additional evidence of the effort John Paul II put into examining this question is the preliminary consultation he held with the presidents of those Bishops' Conferences which were particularly concerned with the problem. All of them without exception declared with full conviction that the Church, out of obedience to the Lord, has no authority to ordain women priests.

Benedict XVI also confirmed this teaching. At Chrisam Mass on 5 April 2012, he recalled how John Paul II declared "irrevocably" that the Church "has received no authority from the Lord with regard to the ordination of women". Benedict XVI then asked himself in view of some who did not accept this teaching: "But is disobedience really a way? Do we sense in it something of the conformation to Christ which is the precondition of every real renewal, or is it not only the desperate urge to do something, to transform the church according to our wishes and ideas?

Pope Francis also commented on this question. In his Apostolic Letter *Evangelii gaudium* he underscored that "the priesthood reserved for men as a sign of Christ, the Bridegroom who gives himself in the Eucharist, is an issue that is not open to discussion". He also called for this teaching to be interpreted not as an expression of power but as service, so that the equal dignity of man and woman in the one Body of Christ may be better understood (n. 104). In the press conference held during the return flight from the

Apostolic Journey to Sweden on 1 November 2016, Pope Francis stressed: "With regard to the consecration of women in the Catholic Church, St. John Paul II has spoken the final clear word, and that remains".

In our time, the Church is called upon to respond to many challenges facing our culture. For this it is essential that it remain in Jesus Christ like the branches on the vine. The Master therefore invites us to keep his words in us: "If you keep my commandments, you will remain in my love" (John 15:10). Only fidelity to His words, which do not pass away, guarantees our rootedness in Christ and in his love. Only the acceptance of his wise plan, which takes shape in the sacraments, strengthens the Church at her roots so that she can bear fruit for eternal life.

Luis F. Ladaria, S.I,
Prefect of the Congregation for the Doctrine of the Faith

I wrote the following press release commenting on this article for the German section of the International Women Priests' Movement (RCWP):

Press release
Re: Vatican affirms "No" to the ordination of women to the priesthood

The current Prefect of the Congregation for the Doctrine of the Faith, Archbishop Luis Ladaria, has in an article published in the Vatican newspaper (30 May 2018) confirmed the "No" to the ordination of women to the priesthood. The allegedly definitive ban on the ordination of women to the priesthood was first pronounced by Pope John Paul II in his Apostolic Letter *Ordinatio Sacerdotalis* (1994).

Since then, this ban has time and again been critically questioned and rejected by reform-minded theologians and women's organizations, and with mounting protest; for "well-founded counter-arguments to the doctrinal position on the ordination of women to the priesthood cannot be brushed aside by simply invoking authority" – no matter how massive it may be (U. Ruh, 1994).

The ban against the ordination of women is ultimately based on harsh, centuries-old discrimination of women, which has not yet been dealt with and overcome by the Vatican Church leadership; (*but*: there are committed people who have already done preparatory work in this direction – see e.g.: http://www.womenpriests.org/de/). Furthermore, the historically critical biblical exegesis has not been used in this decision by the teaching authority; on the other hand, the Pontifical Biblical Commission had already declared in 1976 that the New Testament does not contain any ban on the ordination of women. But all these legitimate insights have been and continue to be ignored by the Church leadership, only to maintain the misogynist patriarchal power structure of the Roman Catholic Church.

But truth will win in the end – and not the lies and continuing discrimination against women. God's holy spiritual power calls upon women and men with a sense of justice in the church to resist this theologically untenable teaching, which runs counter to the urgently needed renewal of the church in the spirit of Jesus Christ; for in Christ, on the basis of faith and baptism, there is "neither male nor female" (Galatians 3:27f), i.e. the difference in rank between the genders and thus the dominion of men over women is finally overcome in Christ.

For the German Section of the International Women Priests' Movement (RCWP): 1 June 2018, *Ida Raming, Dr. theol.*

In an article for the magazine "Kirche In", I rejected the individual reasons forwarded by L. Ladaria against the ordination of women; these remarks can serve as additional information and insight.

"Roma locuta – causa non finita … "
Re.: Ladaria: "Regarding some doubts about the definitive character of the doctrine of *Ordinatio Sacerdotalis*"

The current Prefect of the Congregation for the Doctrine of the Faith, Archbishop Luis Ladaria S.J., in an article in the Vatican newspaper (from 29 May 2018) has reaffirmed the "No" to ordination of women to the priesthood. The allegedly definitive ban on the ordination of women to the priesthood was first pronounced by Pope John Paul II in his Apostolic Letter *Ordinatio Sacerdotalis* (1994).

The reason for this new letter is, according to Ladaria, that "in some countries" voices are being heard "which again call into question the definitive nature of the teachings mentioned". This causes him, the prefect of the Congregation, "great concern".

What reasons does the Prefect of the Congregation for the Doctrine of the Faith give for the allegedly "definitive, infallible doctrine"? – and what are the arguments against it?

1 **"Christ intended to bestow this sacrament (of priestly ordination) on the twelve apostles, who were all men, and they in turn entrusted other men with it. The Church has always been bound by this decision of the Lord, which excludes validly conferring the priesthood of ministry on women … ."**

Counterargument:
Jesus did not administer the sacrament of priestly ordination, but rather sent out apostles to proclaim the Good News of the Kingdom of God.

As a Jew living under the patriarchal structure of Judaism, he could not send out women with the mandate of public proclamation in his time; for women were not allowed to act in public in ancient Israel, e.g. they could not give public testimony in court. Mary Magdalena was told by the Risen Jesus to proclaim the good news: "Go to my brothers", but Jesus could not send her to a synagogue to preach, for example. The male apostles, on the other hand, were able to preach in synagogues.

The Magisterium completely ignores the contemporary situation of women at the time of Jesus, – this is a grave error (non-application of the historical-critical Bible exegesis!). For example, Jesus could not have abolished slavery in his time, either, because it was a social structure – similar to the situation of women.

2. **"The Church has always known that it is bound by this decision (by Christ)..."**

Counterargument:
"Luke and Mt are the only ones who equate the circle of apostles with the circle of the twelve (symbol for the "Twelve Tribes of Israel") but especially in the letters of Paul, the term "apostle" is broader and is oriented towards the testimony of the resurrection" (cf. the statement by Dorothea Sattler under kath.de).

Among these witnesses in the early Church were also women, missionary apostles (e.g. Junia, Priska, etc.). There were also deaconesses, presbyteresses. These early Church ministries of women, which were probably based on Galatians 3:26–28, according to which the biological gender does not play any role (not even in conferring ministry) as a result of faith and baptism, are completely ignored by the teaching authority.

3. **"The Church" has "no authority to ordain women."**

Counter-question and counter-argument:
Does the Church have any explicit command from Jesus *not* to send out women as apostles (or as presbyter women, etc.)? This is not the case; for Jesus did not ever commit women to subordination to men – on the contrary! On several occasions he defended women against men (cf. Luke 13:15f; Mark 14:3–9). He sent Mary Magdalena to proclaim his resurrection to the "brethren"... ! To cite Jesus on this issue is therefore an insult to Jesus.

The church leadership introduced e.g. a cardinalate without the authority of Jesus, who did not specify any structures for the Church; in this case, no question was asked as to whether there was authority from Jesus for such. Other examples could be mentioned... The reference to Jesus, and claim that he did not give authority to send women as apostles, is only a sham argument that is not sustainable.

4. **The priesthood of the ministry requires the male sex of the ordinand for priestly ordination to be valid; "the impossibility of female ordination" is part of the "substance of the sacrament". "The church does not have the power to change this substance." "The priest acts in the person of Christ, the Bridegroom of the church (his "Bride") and his manhood is an indispensable aspect of this sacramental representation..."**

Counter-argument:
Women, by virtue of their personhood and as baptized persons, can act as well as men on behalf of Christ, because in Christ, by virtue of faith and baptism, there is "**neither male nor female**", cf. Galatians 3:26–28: "Since you have been baptized into Christ, **you have clothed yourself in Christ** . . . ", that is, every baptized person, male or female, can act in his name and mission on the basis of their faith in Jesus Christ, the Risen One; this does not require the male gender!

Moreover, there are also other images for the Church, hence not only the "Bride of Christ": For example, "People of God, flock of God . . . ".

Male ministers tend to exclude themselves from the "body of Christ" and to place themselves in Christ's place instead of the "head" of Christ, – but only one is head: Jesus Christ!

5 The "difference in tasks of men and women" means "certainly not subservience, but rather mutual enrichment."

Counterargument:
This statement is pure "whitewashing", obfuscating and trivializing continuing oppression; this is because women are excluded from crucial church offices (priesthood and bishop's office), and hence at the same time also from all decisions relating to church teachings, church law, etc. As oppressed persons, women are subject to clerical male dominance!

6 The "definitive" prohibition of the ordination of women is based (according to Ladaria) on the following understanding of the church's Magisterium: This prohibition is not a "definition ex cathedra", but rather a doctrinal decision by the "Ordinary and General Magisterium of the Bishops scattered throughout the world when they, in communion with each other and with the Pope, present the Catholic doctrine as final and binding". Pope John Paul II was acting according to this principle.

Counterargument and criticism:
Under this understanding on the part of the teaching authority (according to LG No. 25 of the Second Vatican Council), the meaning of "infallibility" has been expanded. This expansion was rightly sharply criticized by lawyers and canonists at the time (e.g. L. Örsy). The example of the ban on the ordination of women clearly illustrates the justified criticism of this:
- **sensus fidelium** (the sense of faith of the people of God) has not been put in question;
- **exclusively men** (Pope and Bishops, i.e. the presidents of the Bishops' Conferences) **rendered judgment on the status of women**, – men who, because of their education and as representatives of the clergy, consider themselves to be rulers over women, who consider the supremacy of men over women to

be a "divine order of creation" and **thus violate the spirit of Jesus Christ, who expressly said: "Not so with you!** (Mathew 20, 26–28).
This means that the prohibition of female ordination is deeply unjust and contradicts the spirit of Jesus Christ. Furthermore, it is theologically untenable. Therefore the denunciation and rejection of this allegedly "final" truth, which purportedly "is one of the elements of Church belief", will not disappear in the future. This is required in terms of the personal dignity of women and the calling upon women to assume priestly ministry – a calling which does not come from the Church, but rather the holy spiritual power of God!

Possibly for the first time in the history of the Church there is an opportunity not only to shake the foundations upon which this allegedly definitive doctrinal decision stands, but also to fundamentally counter and repudiate the hubris that church officials have taken upon themselves in proclaiming doctrines rife with errors to be "infallible".

Prof. Hermann Häring issues a plea in his engaging article **"A toxic threat. The discussion surrounding purportedly infallible statements"** (published on the website of Wir sind Kirche at http://www.wir-sind-kirche.de) to make criticism of so-called "infallibility" the core aim in all reform efforts. For, in his words, this presumed infallibility serves as a "general obstacle" thwarting all necessary reforms.

This has indeed been the painful lesson experienced by anyone striving for necessary church reforms.

For Christians, then, it is only trust and faith in the holy spiritual power of God that should be binding, as this "will lead us into all truth" (John 14, 25f and 16, 14); i.e. **we human beings/Christians are only on the path to knowledge of the truth** and cannot proclaim truths that are binding for all times and make these binding on people.

In June 2018
Ida Raming, Dr theol.

- **In closing: My (not always successful) experiences in the struggle:**

From several sides, especially from fellow compatriots struggling for complete equality of women in the Roman Catholic Church, I have repeatedly heard the complaint that women do not stand up in solidarity for women called upon to enter the priestly ministry – often enough citing the argument: "*I do not want to become a priest!*" It would appear that these persons are indifferent to how women are generally perceived and treated in their church.

Obviously the long history of discrimination against women in the Catholic Church, which has yet to be overcome, has left deep scars on women (lack of self-esteem as women, lack of honor and dignity ...). In this sense, there is still a real need for intensive healing and educational work to be done – a task which could especially be assumed by "sisters in the priestly ministry".

In all these efforts, I believe in the power of truth:

"Truth will prevail in the end – not lies!"

Bibliographical reference:

I. Raming:

Article: *The all too long history of discrimination against women because of their gender – this has not yet been overcome and is still having a seriously negative impact on the Roman Catholic Church! Patriarchalism urgently needs to be banished!*

(The article has been published in the journal "Imprimatur". News and critical opinions from the Catholic Church, year 48, no. 3, 2015, pp. 162–166)

My appeal to all (Catholic) women:

Our struggle for access to all services and ministries in the Catholic Church involves no less than
- full recognition of the personal dignity of women, their human rights (which includes freedom of choice of profession, etc.)!
- recognition and acknowledgement of the spiritual vocations of women through God's holy spiritual power, "which is given to everyone as she/he wills" (1 Corinthians 12:11)
- your/our freedom as daughters of God!
- a fundamental renewal of the church in the spirit of Jesus Christ, which cannot be achieved without the active cooperation and equality of women!
  Hence my call: My dear sisters! Embrace your responsibility for this important task!

May 2018
Ida Raming, Dr. theol.

PS. The film-maker **Gerhard Stahl** has produced a film about our long struggle since the Second Vatican Council: **"Zur Priesterin berufen"** (Ida Raming).

This film is expressly recommended for teaching purposes by the Landesmedien-Zentrum Baden-Württemberg.

VI   Note with a view to current events

It is evident throughout the entire world: The Roman Catholic Church is embroiled in a profound crisis, both due to the ghastly sexual abuse scandal which was covered up for so long, but also because of the centuries of suppression and discrimination against women in the church – with this half of church members being excluded from all ordained ministries. This is also intimately connected with an additional area of crisis: the inferior status of lay people in the church predominantly resulting from the hierarchical structure of the Roman Catholic Church.

Ever since the profound crisis of the Church broke into the public sphere, a virtual uprising has developed over the last few years in several countries, including Germany:

Organisations of lay people, women's organisations and, finally, bishops as well have now together called a **"Synodal Path"** (Synodaler Weg), which recently commenced at the end of January/beginning of February 2020.

A description of some of the aims and objectives of this "Synodal Path" from a German source translated by Christian Weisner are provided in the following (Wir sind Kirche.de):

Information in English

The Synodal Path – The history (English translation: Christian Weisner, Wir sind Kirche.de)

The Spring Plenary Assembly of the German Bishops' Conference from 11 to 14 March 2019 in Lingen was influenced by the so-called MHG study (Research Project "Sexual abuse of minors by catholic priests, deacons and male members of orders in the domain of the German Bishops' Conference") on the survey of cases of sexual abuse in the domain of the Catholic Church, which had already shaped the Autumn Plenary Assembly in September 2018.

In the period up to spring 2019, the German bishops in the meetings of the Permanent Council had repeatedly dealt with the question of the consequences of the MHG study. Already in September 2018, the Plenary Assembly declared: "The challenges specific to the Catholic Church, such as the questions of the celibate way of life of priests and various aspects of Catholic sexual morality, will be discussed in a transparent process of dialogue with experts from various disciplines."

A study day during the Plenary Assembly in Lingen took up questions from the MHG study. Its theme was: "Die Frage nach der Zäsur – Studientag zu übergreifenden Fragen, die sich gegenwärtig stellen" ("The question of the turning-point-study day on overarching questions that currently arise"). The lectures given there were published on dbk.de.

In Lingen it became obvious: shock waves require special procedures. The MHG-study and, as a result, the demand of many for reforms show: the Church in Germany is experiencing a turning point. Faith can only grow and deepen if one becomes free from thinking blockades, if one faces up to the free and open debate and develops the ability to take new positions and to go new ways.

The decision concerning the Synodal Path

For this reason, in Lingen the decision was taken to follow a Synodal Path. The conviction was expressed: the Church needs synodal progress. Pope Francis recommends it. Even the Church in Germany does not start from the beginning. The "Joint Synod of the Dioceses of the Federal Republic of Germany" ("Würzburg Synod", 1971 to 1975), the "Pastoral Synod of the Catholic Church in the GDR" (1973 – 1975) and also the discussion process of the past years have prepared the ground, also for many challenges of today. Cardinal Reinhard Marx declared in the closing press conference of the Lingen Plenary Assembly that it had been decided "to follow a binding Synodal Path as the Church in Germany, which makes possible a structured debate and takes place in an agreed period of time, together with the Central Committee of German Catholics (ZdK). We will create formats for open debates and commit ourselves to procedures that enable the responsible participation of women and men from our dioceses. We want to be a listening Church. We need the advice of people outside the Church".

In addition, Cardinal Marx explained which aspects will be important as regards the Synodal Path:
"We know about the cases of the clerical abuse of power. It betrays the trust of people in search of stability and religious orientation. What must be done to achieve the necessary reduction of power and establish a more just and legally binding order will be clarified by the Synodal Path. The establishment of administrative courts is part of this.
We know that the way of life of bishops and priests demands changes in order to show the inner freedom of faith and the orientation towards the example of Jesus Christ. We value celibacy as an expression of the religious relationship with God.

We will find out how far it must belong to the witness of the priest in our Church. The sexual morality of the Church has not yet absorbed decisive insights from theology and human sciences. The personal meaning of sexuality does not receive sufficient attention. The result: the proclamation of morality does not give orientation to the vast majority of the baptized. It leads a niche existence. We sense how often we are not able to speak when it comes to questions about today's sexual behavior".

The deliberations of the Central Committee of German Catholics

During its Plenary Assembly on 10 – 11 May 2019 in Mainz, the Central Committee of German Catholics (ZdK) dealt with the issue of the Synodal Path of the Church in Germany. With a clear majority, the Assembly voted to help shape this path constructively. The Committee and the Main Committee were instructed by the Plenary Assembly to continue the planning with the German Bishops' Conference in binding cooperation and under common leadership, to provide the necessary personnel and financial means for this and to ensure the networking of the representatives of the ZdK.

The following four forums have been set up for the work of the Synodal Way:
- Power and separation of powers in the Church – Joint participation and sharing in mission (originally: "power and separation of powers") > members
- Priestly existence today (originally: "priestly way of life") > members
- Women in Church Services and Ministry > members
- Living in successful relationships – practicing love in sexuality and partnership (originally: "sexual morals") > members

What happens next?
The Synodal Assemblies will take place from 30 January to 1 February 2020 and from 3 to 5 September 2020 (delayed because of "Corona") in Frankfurt/Main.
Documents
Here we document the most important texts in the preparation of the Synodal Path and the Statutes of the Synodal Path.
Downloads & Infos
- Statutes of the Synodal Path

Read more about how the Synodal Path is organised.
Download pdf
- FAQ

Get more answers in our Frequently Asked Questions (English)
Download pdf
- Letter of Cardinal Marx and Prof. Dr Sternberg

The President of the German Bishops' Conference, Cardinal Reinhard Marx, and the President of the Central Committee of German Catholics (ZdK), Prof. Dr Thomas Sternberg, wrote a letter to the faithful in Germany on 1 December 2019 (published 27/11/2019).

Press release from WOW in February 2020 **in response to Pope Francis "Amazon text":**
For Immediate Release.
Press Contacts:
- Kate McElwee (USA/Italy): +39 393 692 2100; kmcelwee@womensordination.org
- Miriam Duignan (UK/Ireland): +44 7970 926910; miriam.duignan@wijngaardsinstitute.com
- Alicja Baranowska(Belgium & Poland): +32 488 67 60 20 alicja.baranowska@wp.pl
- Therese Koturbash (Canada): +1 204 648 5720; t.m.koturbash@gmail.com

Reading the post-synodal document, WOW concludes that it is on the back of a crucified Christ imaged in the faces of women that Pope Francis proposes to continue running the Roman Catholic man show. Turning his back on a significant opportunity to make a breakthrough for women, Francis has opted to perpetuate the shameful elitist man club that, as he so brazenly points out in the document, is held up by the second class status of women who do most of the work with none of the recognition.

Despite his concern for the environment and global climate catastrophe, Francis utterly fails to connect the marginalisation of the environment (a *'she'*) with the marginalisation of the feminine in the world and in particular, the *'she'* who is marginalised in our own Church. Astonishingly, Francis holds up defense of the all-male priesthood on the untenable foundation of spousal imagery that says priest stands in for groom and the Church as bride. In application, this practice dramatically underlines how men can fill all the roles through a gender fluid pansexuality granted for male priests. While the male priest stands in for groom, he also and stands in for bride. Women in this broken view are but passive recipients in the source and summit of our faith. Women are categorically unnecessary for the function of the Church except for the production of children and to prop up the man show. This theory betrays a blind belief in a concept called *complementarity* used by the Vatican to claim that women and men are destined for different roles but which in reality just means men can do everything and women can only do what the men want them to and that serves them.

His rejection of women in ministerial service is nothing less than a betrayal of the entire faith community that waits desperately in need of culturally competent priests. God calls women to priesthood and to the diaconate. When an informed examination is made of the Vatican's efforts to justify excluding women from sacred ministry, it is clear that:
- there is no reason in scripture, theology, or the tradition of the Church to support a male only priesthood. This is evidenced in the huge body of studies available on the academic website womenpriests.org;
- for century after century, the hierarchy has fed prejudice against women to the faithful as though it were truth. This prejudice underpins the Vatican's official rationale for excluding women from priesthood and the diaconate. Through his Post Synodal Apostolic Exhortation on the Amazon region Pope Francis insists on perpetuating it.

Pope Francis, it is long past time for your boys' club to recognise that women are not *'other'* but are fully human. The continued exclusion of the woman from priesthood is flagrant injustice that harms the Church and signals to the world that it is ok to continue treating women as less than. In this scenario there can be little sympathy for a leadership who fumbles with the inevitable emptying of pews and deconsecration of growing numbers of Catholic churches.

As things stand now, the Church remains a man's Church where women are permitted to worship, to deliver goods and services and to be stamped with something less than the icons of Christ that we fully, wholly, truly and completely are.

Founded in 1996, **Women's Ordination Worldwide (WOW)** is an international network of groups whose current mission is to see Catholic women admitted to all ordained ministries in the Church. WOW is founded on the gospel principle of equality and therefore opposes any discrimination. 'There is neither Jew nor Greek, there is no longer slave or free, there is no long male and female for you are all one in Christ Jesus' (Galatians 3:28).

Voices of Faith – Press release:
Inspired by Amazonia women, we take on responsibility – a CWC statement to Querida Amazonia
February 13, 2020
Rome, 13 February 2020

Yesterday the post-synodal exhortation "Querida Amazonia" was published. With great sensitivity, it discussed the problems of poverty, exploitation, cultural colonization, migration and environmental degradation the Amazonia region is currently facing. It encouraged dialogue and appreciation of the unique contribution of the indigenous peoples to the shape of the universal Church.

What was most striking from the exhortation was that it did not resolve the great dilemmas brought to the Vatican by the preparatory document to the Synod. Instead, it seemed this document served as a further withdrawal from any concrete or bold proposals for reform and to bring about solutions to the pressing issues the Amazonia region are facing. The Pope recommended reading the final document of the Synod but did not settle the questions and open pastoral suggestions contained therein. "Querida Amazonia" proposed no concrete answers or solutions to those questions and requests.

One of the key issues brought to the Vatican by the Amazon Church was the formal recognition of women's ministry and the possible sacramental support for their dedicated service in the Church. However, instead of concrete new proposals and solutions, there were a mere five paragraphs entitled "The strength and gift of women".

In this section, the Pope writes about the great work, often indispensable, that women do in the Amazon Church, although that work is not formally recognized. Sadly, this appreciation of the role of women not only perpetuates but reinforces the exclusive tradition of the Church's designation of a "special" place for women. This tradition describes women in a romanticized and idealized way, suggesting their role is in some way exceptional and set apart from or above and beyond the human norm. As a consequence, the basic form, the subject of Christian anthropology and moral theology, is man, and woman continues to be assigned a "special", unique task, which does not include the diversity, freedom and charisms reserved for the "basic" version.

The shocking expression of this mentality is outlined in point 101 of the exhortation. The Pope writes that God has shown God's power and love through two human faces: Christ and Mary. By putting them side by side, he is suggesting that men are similar to the former (Christ) and women to the latter (Mary). This takes away from the teaching that both woman and man are created in the image of God and thus both are, can and should be "Alter Christus".

The theology behind this phrase is dangerous because it serves to exclude women from access to the full means of salvation. For there is an important ontological difference between Jesus and Mary – even though they are both human, Jesus is also God. The basis of the Christian faith is the conviction that Christ adopted human nature inclusively, not male nature exclusively, and that thanks to this, every human being can be saved and is indeed divinized in Christ.

So, if women are only being compared to the likeness of Mary, then why are women baptized in the name of Christ? Why at baptism are they called to be priestly, prophetic and royal which is a share in Christ's own priestly, prophetic and royal ministry? How should they understand the term "Imitatio Christi", which is so fundamental to any Christian spirituality? Above all, on what basis are they to be saved if they do not share the likeness of Christ?

At the same time, there remains, of course, the practical question of what this "characteristic power" is that women in the Church have. The document seems to suggest that it consists in imitating Mary's motherhood. How should this be understood? How should it be manifested concretely for the community of believers? If we are to take it seriously, is the evaluation and thus validity of our vocations and charisms to be verified only by their similarity to motherhood?

Moreover, the document offers a compelling vision of an inculturated priesthood suffused by the values of pastoral care. But surely, if clericalism is a dysfunctional aspect of the contemporary priesthood and inculturation offers a new and more diverse understanding of what it means to be a priest, then the ordination of women with all the qualities that Pope Francis attributes to them would be the best possible antidote to the clerical mindset?

Most of the document speaks with great respect and maturity about the indigenous people of the Amazon, about their needs and concerns. It encourages the global Church to listen to their opinions and their stories with sensitivity and attention. What is striking is the contrast with which women are treated in the very same document – their voices have so clearly not been heard, they are not equal partners for shaping the future of the Church.

In spite of this clearly excluding message we, women from Catholic Women's Council will not give up our hopes and vocations. Inspired by the example of our Amazonian sisters in faith, and in imitation of the Syrophoenician woman who persisted despite Jesus' initial rebuff (Mark 7:25–30), we take responsibility for our Church into our hands. United we will work for the Church that incarnates the equality and dignity we find in the Gospel and that teaches us to follow Christ whoever we are.

Organisations:

AGENDA Forum katholischer Theologinnen e.V.
Catholic Women Speak
Donne per la Chiesa
FrauenKirche Zentralschweiz
Friends of Catholic Women's Ordination
Future Church
In Bona Fide
KDFB
KDFB – Bundesverband
Katholische Frauengemeinschaft Deutschlands (kfd)
Maria 2.0

Noi siamo Chiesa
Order of Franciscans of the Eucharist – Order of Franciscans Ecumenical
Spazio Asmara – Busto Arsizio
Voices of Faith
We Are Church Ireland
Women and the Australian Church (WATAC)
Women's Ordination Conference

Individuals: (a lot of indiviuals undersigned the press release) …
About Catholic Women's Council (CWC):

The Catholic Women's Council was first formed in Stuttgart in November 2019, when Catholic women's associations, initiatives, women religious orders and church bodies from Germany, Austria, Liechtenstein and Switzerland came together to network on a united position of women in the Church for the very first time. In January 2020, this network became global as an umbrella group. We invite other groups to join this coalition.

Media contact
For interviews please contact Voices of Faith General Manager, Zuzanna Flisowska.
zuzanna.flisowska@voicesoffaith.org + 39 351 523 4217
To learn more about Voices of Faith, please visit: https://voicesoffaith.org

Appendix: Bibliographie

The following is a bibliography of English- and French-language sources in chronological order according to year of publication.

1973/74

Heyer, Robert J., ed. Women and Orders. New York: Paulist Press, 1974.
King, J.A. "The Ordination of Women to the Priesthood." Theology 78 (1974): 142–147.
Morris, Joan. Against Nature and God. The History of Women with Clerical Ordination and the Jurisdiction of Bishops. London: Mowbrays, 1973.

1975

Carroll, Elizabeth. "Women and Ministry." Theological Studies 36 (1975): 660–687.
Donnelly, Dorothy H. "Women-Priests – Does Philadelphia Have a Message for Rome?" Commonweal 102 (1975): 206–210.
Hamilton, Michael P. and Nancy S. Montgomery, eds. The Ordination of Women: Pro and Con. New York: Morehouse-Barlow Co., 1975.
Lakeland, Paul. Can Women Be Priests. Ordination of Women in Ecumenical Perspective. Cork: The Mercier Press, 1975.
Meyer, Eric C. "Are There Theological Reasons Why the Church Should not Ordain Women Priests?" Review for Religious 34 (1975): 957–967.

1976

Bouyer, Louis. Mystère et ministères de la femme. Paris: Aubier Montaigne, 1976.
Bruce, Michael and Gervase E. Duffield, eds. Why not? Priesthood and the Ministry of Women: A Theological Study. Abington, PA: Marcham Manor Press,

1976.

Gardiner, Anne Marie, ed. Women and Catholic Priesthood. An Expanded Vision. New York: Paulist Press, 1976.

Micks, Marianne and Charles P. Price. Towards a New Theology of Ordination. Essays on the Ordination of Women. Sommerville, MA: Hadden &Company Ltd., 1976.

1977

Coridin, James A., ed. Sexism and Church Law. New York: Paulist Press, 1977.

Swidler, Leonard and Arlene Swidler, eds. Women Priests. A Catholic Commentary on the Vatican Declaration. New York: Paulist Press, 1977.

Wijngaards, John. Did Christ Rule Out Women Priests? Great Wakering: Mayhew_McCrimmon, 1977.

1978

Coyle, John K. "The Fathers on Women's Ordination." Eglise et Théologie 9 (1978): 51–101.

di Noia, Joseph. "Women's Ordination: can the Debate Be Revived?" New Black Friars 59 (1978): 488–497.

Ferder, Fran. Called to Break Bread?: A Psychological Investigation of 100 Women Who Feel Called to Priesthood in the Catholic Church. Mt. Ranier, MD: Quixote Center, 1978.

Hemperek, Piotr. "The Catholic Church and the Ordination of Women." Roczniki teologiczno-kanoniczne 25 (1978): 33–44.

Stuhlmueller, Carroll, ed. Women and the Priesthood: Future Directions. Collegeville, MN: The Liturgical Press, 1978.

1979

Singles, Donna. "The Case of Women in the Church: Objection Sustained." Concilium 15 (1979): 71–79.

1980

Brennan, Margaret. "Women and Men in Church Office." Concilium 16 (1980): 107–109.

Parvey, Constance F., ed. Ordination of Women in Ecumenical Perspective. Commission on Faith and Order. Geneva: World Council of Churches, 1980.

Ordination of Women in Ecumenical Perspective: Workbook for the Church's Future. Geneva: World Council of Churches, 1980.

1981

Bébère, Marie-Jeanne. "L'ordination des femmes." Lumière et vie 30 (1981): 90–102.

1982

Warkentin, Marjorie. Ordination. A Biblical-Historical Overview. Grand Rapids, MI: Eerdmans, 1982.

1984

Doyle, Eric. "The Question of Women Priests and the Argument In Persona Christi.' Irish Theological Quarterly 37 (1984): 212–221.

1986

Wijngaards, John. Did Christ Rule Out Women Priests?, 2nd ed. Essex: McCrimmons, 1986.
Women Priests, Obstacles to Unity? Documents and Correspondence Rome and Canterbury 1975–1986. London: Catholic Truth Society, 1986.

1987

Martin, John H. "The Injustice of Not Ordaining Women: A Problem for Medieval Theologians." Theological Studies 48 (1987): 303–316.
Rosato, Philip J. "Priesthood of the Baptized and Priesthood of the Ordained." Gregorianum 68 (1987): 215–265.

1988

Osborne, Kenan B. Priesthood: A History of the Ordained Ministry in the Roman Catholic Church. New York: Paulist Press, 1988.

1989

Field, Barbara, ed. Fit for this Office. Women and Ordination. Melbourne: Collins Dove, 1989.
Trapp, Daniel J. The Discussion of the Ordination of Women to the Priesthood among Roman Catholics in the United States 1977–1987. Rome: Graziani, 1989.

1991

Behr-Seigel, Elisabeth. Le minstère de la femme dans L'Eglise. Paris: Editions du Cerf., 1991.

1993

Armstrong, Karen. The End of Silence: Women and the Priesthood. London: Fourth Estate, 1993.
Légrand, Hervé. "Traditio Perpetuo Servata? The Non-Ordination of Women: Tradition or Simply Historical Fact?" One in Christ 29 (1993): 1–23.

1994

Byrne, Lavinia. Women at the Altar – The Ordination of Women in the Roman Catholic Church. London: Mowbray, 1994.
Cullinane, Peter J. "Bischof, A Pastoral-Theological Reflection on Pope John Paul II's Apostolic Letter Concerning Ordination to the Priesthood." Australasian Catholic Record 71 (1994): 465–474.
St. Pierre, Simone M. The Struggle to Serve: The Ordination of Women in the Roman Catholic Church. Jefferson, NC: McFarland, 1994.
Waldrond-Skinner, Sue. Crossing the Boundary. What Will Women Priests Mean? London: Mowbray, 1994.

1995

Dulles, Avery. "Tradition Says No." The Tablet 249 (1995): 1572–1573.
Glesson, Gerald. "The Status of the Church's Teaching that Ordination is Reserved to Men Alone." The Australasian Catholic Record 73 (1995): 286–294.
McSorley, Harry. "Ecclesial Communio, Reception, and the Apostolic Letter of Pope John Paul II. '*Ordinatio Sacerdotalis*'." Communion et Réunion (1995): 389–401.
Reynolds, Philip R. "Scholastic Theology and the Case Against Women's Ordination." Heythrop Journal 36 (1995): 249–285.
Sullivan, Francis A., S.J. "Guideposts from Catholic Tradition. Infallibility Doctrine Invoked in Statement against Ordination by Congregation for the Doctrine of Faith." America 173:9 (1995): 5–6.

1996

Bébère, Marie-Jeanne. "L'ordination des femmes dans L'Eglise catholique: Les decisions du magistère." Revue de droit canonique 46 (1996): 7–20.

Catholic Theological Society of America. "Tradition and Women's Ordination: A Question for Criteria." Origins 26 (1996): 556–564.
Eisen, Ute E. Amtsträgerinnen im frühen Christentum. Epigraphische und literarische Studien. Göttingen: Vandenhoeck & Ruprecht, 1996. English translation: Women Officeholders in Early Christianity. Epigraphical and Literary Studies. Collegeville, MN: The Liturgical Press, 2000.
Ferme, Brian E. "The Response of the Congregation for the Doctrine of Faith to the Dubium Concerning the Apostolic Letter' Ordinatio Sacerdotalis': Authority and Significance." Periodica 85 (1996) 689–727.
Field-Bibb, Jacqueline. "Praxis versus Image: Women Towards the Priesthood in the Roman Catholic Church." Concilium 32 (1996): 81–89.
Gaillardetz, Richard R. "Infallibility and the Ordination of Women." Louvain Studies 21 (1996): 3–24.
Joubert, Jacques. "L'ordination des femmes et le depot de la foi. A propos d'une 'résponse' de la Congrégation pour la doctrine de la foi." Revue de droit canonique 46 (1996): 29–36.
Sullivan, Francis A., S.J. Creative Fidelity: Weighing and Interpreting Documents of Magisterium. New York: Paulist Press, 1996.

1998

Gössman, Elisabeth. "Women's Ordination and the Vatican." Feminist Theology 18 (1998): 67–86.
van Lunen Chénu, Marie-Thérèse. "Human Rights in the Church: a non-right for women in the Church." Human Rights. The Christian Contribution (1998).

1999

The Non-Ordination of Women and the Politics of Power. Concilium 35, n. 3. Elisabeth Schüssler Fiorenza and Hermann Häring, eds. Maryknoll, NY: Orbis Books,1999.
Berlis, Angela. "The Ordination of Women: A Test Case for Conciliarity." Unanswered questions. Concilium 35, n 1. Christoph Theobald and Dietmar Mieth, eds. Maryknoll, NY: Orbis Books,1999. 77–84.

2000

Macy, Gary. "The Ordination of Women in the Early Middle Ages." Theological Studies 61 (2000): 481–507.
Raab, Kelley A. When Women Become Priests. New York: Columbia University Press, 2000.

2001

Wijngaards, John. The Ordination of Women in the Catholic Church. Unmasking a Cuckoo's Egg Tradition. London: Mowbray, 2001.

Winter, Miriam T. Out of the Depths. The Story of Ludmila Javorova, Ordained Roman Catholic Priest. New York: Crossroad Publishing Co., 2001.

2005

Blohm, Uta: Religious traditions and personal stories: women working as priests, ministers and rabbis, Frankfurt: Lang 2005

2010

Raming, Ida / Müller, Iris: 'Contra Legem'. Our lifelong Struggle for Human Rights for Women in the Roman Catholic Church, Berlin: LIT Verlag 2010

2016

Straub, Jaqueline: Jung, katholisch, weiblich. Weshalb ich Priesterin werden will. Oberursel: Publik-Forum Verlagsgesellschaft, 2016. (Englische Übersetzung: Fisher King Publishing Ltd., England 2017)

2017

Taddel-Ferret, Cloe: Even the Dogs: The Ordination of Women in the Catholic Church. Berlin: LIT Verlag 2017.

German-language sources are provided in the following, also in chronological order according to years:

1973/74

Raming, Ida, Der Ausschluss der Frau vom priesterlichen Amt. Gottgewollte Tradition oder Diskriminierung? Köln: Böhlau Verlag 1973

1975

Raming, Ida. "Frau und kirchliche Ämter." 24–28 in Diaconia Christi. Dokumentation, edited by Internationales Diakonatszentrum Freiburg, 1975.

1976

Küng, Hans. "Thesen zur Stellung der Frau in Kirche und Gesellschaft." Theologische Quartalschrift 156 (1976): 129–132.

Neumann, Johannes. "Die Stellung der Frau in der Sicht der katholischen Kirche heute." Theologische Quartalschrift 156 (1976): 111–128.

Radford, Rosemary R. "Frau und kirchliches Amt in historischer und gesellschaftlicher Sicht." Concilium 12 (1976): 17–23.

Raming, Ida. "Die inferiore Stellung der Frau nach geltendem Kirchenrecht." Concilium 12 (1976): 30–34.

Schüssler, Elisabeth F. "Die Rolle der Frau in der urchristlichen Bewegung." Concilium 12 (1976): 3–9.

1977

Ebneter, Albert. "Keine Frauen im Priesteramt." Orientierung 41 (1977): 25f. Freiling, Reinhard. "Rom gegen Frauenordination. Belastung für die Ökumene."

Lutherische Monatshefte 16 (1977): 130f.

Hünermann, Peter. "Roma locuta – causa finita? Zur Argumentation der vatikanischen Erklärung über die Frauenordination." Herder Korrespondenz 31 (1977): 206–209.

Küng, Hans and Gerhard Lohfink. "Keine Ordination der Frau?" Theologische Quartalschrift 157 (1977): 144–146.

Rahner, Karl. "Priestertum der Frau?" Stimmen der Zeit 195 (1977): 291–201.

Sekretariat d. Dt. Bischofskonferenz, ed. Erklärung der Kongregation für die Glaubenslehre zur Frage der Zulassung der Frauen zum Priesteramt. Bonn: Sekretariat d. Dt. Bischofskonferenz, 1977.

Weger, Karl-Heinz. "Endgültig keine Ordination der Frau?" Orientierung 41 (1977): 64–67.

1978

Bläser, Peter. "Liturgische Dienste und die Ordination von Frauen in nichtkatholischen Kirchen." Liturgisches Jahrbuch 28 (1978): 155–169.

1979

Pissarek-Hudelist, Herlinde. "Die Bedeutung der Sakramententheologie Karl Rahners für die Diskussion um das Priestertum der Frau." 417–434 in Wagnis Theologie. Erfahrungen mit der Theologie Karl Rahners, edited by Herbert Vorgrimler. Freiburg: Herder, 1979.

Raming, Ida. "Gleichwertig – aber andersartig". Zu einem üblichen Argumentationsschema gegen das Priestertum der Frau." Orientierung 43 (1979): 218–221.

1980

Reichle, Erika. "Frauenordination aus ökumenischer Sicht. Ein Bericht über eine Tagung." Ökumenische Rundschau 29 (1980): 89–96.

1982

Brooten, Bernadette and Norbert Greinacher, eds. Frauen in der Männerkirche. München: Kaiser, 1982.
Gemeinsame römisch-Katholische Evangelisch-Lutherische Kommission, ed. Das geistliche Amt in der Kirche. Paderborn: Verlag Bonifatius-Druckerei, 1982.
Hauke, Manfred. Die Problematik um das Frauenpriestertum vor dem Hintergrund der Schöpfungs-und Erlösungsordnung. Paderborn: Verlag Bonifatius- Druckerei, 1982.
Legrand, Hervé and Jorge Vikström. "Die Zulassung der Frau zum Amt." 102–126 in: Das geistliche Amt in der Kirch, edited by Gemeinsame
römisch-Katholische Evangelisch-Lutherische Kommission. Paderborn: Verlag Bonifatius-Druckerei, 1982.

1983

Nientiedt, Klaus. "Verdrängte Weiblichkeit. Zur Stellung der Frau in der Kirche." Herder Korrespondenz 37 (1983): 573–578.
Puza, Richard. "Zur Stellung der Frau im alten und neuen Kirchenrecht." Theologische Quartalschrift 163 (1983): 109–122.

1984

"Die Ordination der Frau in Lutherischen Kirchen. Ergebnisse einer Umfrage des Lutherischen Weltbundes." LWB-Dokumentation 18 (1984): 1–39.
Pree, Helmuth. "Mann und Frau im neuen Kirchenrecht." Diakonia 15 (1984): 107–112.
Raming, Ida. "Damit auch Frauen Priester werden... Die Women's Ordination Conference streitet für mehr Rechte der Frauen in der Kirche." Publik-Forum 13:10 (1984): 26f.
Schelkle, Karl H. "'Denn wie das Weib aus dem Mann ist, so auch der Mann aus dem Weib' (1 Kor 11, 12). Zur Gleichberechtigung der Frau in Neuen Testament." Diakonia 15 (1984): 85–90.

1985

Jensen, Anne. "Wie patriarchalisch ist die Ostkirche/ Frauenfragen in der orthodoxen Theologie." Una Sancta 40 (1985): 130–145.
Oeyen, Christian. "Frauenordination: Was sagt die Tradition wirklich?" Internationale Kirchliche Zeitschrift 75 (1985): 97–118.
Parvey, Constance F., ed. Die Gemeinschaft von Frauen und Männern in der Kirche. Neukirchen-Vluyn: Neukirchener Verlag, 1985.
Ruh, Ulrich. "Anglikanische Entscheidung für die Frauenordination." Herder Korrespondenz 39 (1985): 12f.

1986

Heinzelmann, Gertrud. Die geheiligte Diskriminierung: Beiträge zum kirchlichen Feminismus. Bonstetten: Interfeminas, 1986.
Oeyen, Christian. "Priesteramt der Frau? Die altkatholische Theologie als Beispiel einer Denkentwicklung." Ökumenische Rundschau 35 (1986): 254–266.
Ruh, Ulrich. "Anglikaner: Streit um Frauenordination und Glaubensfragen." Herder Korrespondenz 40 (1986): 361f.

1987

Beinert, Wolfgang, ed. Frauenbefreiung und Kirche: Darstellung – Analyse – Dokumentation. Regensburg: F. Pustet, 1987.
Bührig, Marga. "Wenn Frauen Heilige sein können, warum können sie nicht auch Priesterinnen sein?" Reformatio 36 (1987): 331–334.
Gössmann, Elisabeth and Dietmar Bader, eds. Warum keine Ordination der Frau? Unterschiedliche Einstellungen in den christlichen Kirchen. München: Schnell & Steiner, 1987.
Hauke, Manfred. "Das Weihesakrament für Frauen – eine Forderung der Zeit?" Forum Katholische Theologie 3 (1987): 119–134.
Kaufmann, Ludwig. "Auf dem Weg zur Teilhabe." Orientierung 51 (1987): 144.
Vögtle, Anton. "Frauen und Ämter in der frühen Kirche." Christ in der Gegenwart 39 (1987): 389–405.

1988

"Ein Plädoyer für die Frau im kirchlichen Amt. Die Enzyklika "Mulieris dignitatem' über die Würde der Frau." Imprimatur 21 (1988): 322–324.
Lissner, Anneliese. Zur Gleichheit berufen: Entwurf des "Frauen"-Hirtenbriefes der Katholischen Bischofskonferenz der USA. Oberursel: Publik-Forum,

1988. Nürnberg, Rosemarie. "'Non decet neque necessarium est, ut mulieres doceant.' Überlegungen zum altkirchlichen Lehrverbot für Frauen." JAC 31 (1988): 57–73.
Raming, Ida. "Frauenordination. Fortschritt auf dem Weg zur Befreiung der Frau in der katholischen Kirche." Schlangenbrut 22 (1988): 10–14.
Raske, Michael. "Warum dürfen Frauen nicht Priester werden?" Katechetische Blätter 113 (1988): 886–895.
Wojciechowski, Tadeusz. "Könnte eine Frau katholischer Priester sein?" Analecta Cracoviensia 20 (1988): 299–308.

1989

"Beschluß der 49. ordentlichen Bistumssynode der Altkatholiken zur Frauenordination." Ökumenische Rundschau 38 (1989): 333.
"Die Stellung der Frau in der Orthodoxen Kirche und die Frage der Ordination von Frauen. Abschlußbericht einer Interorthodoxen Theologischen Konsultation." Una Sancta 44 (1989): 252–260.
Gössman, Elisabeth. "Außerungen zum Frauenpriestertum in der christlichen Tradition." 304–321 in Freiburger Akademiearbeiten 1979–1989, edited by Dietmar Bader. München: Schnell & Steiner, 1989.

1990

'Gleiche Würde' – aber keine gleichen Rechte. Stellungnahme der Frauengruppe Maria von Magdala zum Apostolischen Schreiben Johannes Pauls II. Mulieris Dignitatem." 46–51 in: Es gibt nicht mehr Mann und Frau ... (Gal 3,28), edited by Initiative Gleichberechtigung für Frauen in der Kirche, 1990.
Raming, Ida and Iris Müller. "Testfall 'Frauenordination'. Amtskirchliche Positionen und ihre Widerlegung." 13–18 in: Es gibt nicht mehr Mann und Frau ... (Gal 3,28), edited by Initiative Gleichberechtigung für Frauen in der Kirche, 1990.
Raming, Ida. "Frauen in der Kirche." Stimmen der Zeit 115 (1990) 415–426.

1991

Raming, Ida. Frauenbewegung und Kirche. Bilanz eines 25jährigen Kampfes für Gleichberechtigung und Befreiung der Frau seit dem 2. Vatikanischen Konzil, 2nd ed. Weinheim: Dt. Studien Verlag, 1991.

1992

Baumert, Norbert. Frau und Mann bei Paulus. Überwindung eines Mißverständnisses. Würzburg: Echter, 1992.
Geldbach, Erich. "Frauenordination: Dienst an der Ökumene?" Materialdienst des Konfessionskundlichen Instituts Bensheim 43 (1992): 103–107.
Kirchenamt der Evangelischen Kirche in Deutschland, ed. Frauenordination und Bischofsamt: eine Stellungnahme der Kammer für Theologie. Hannover: Kirchenamt der Evangelischen Kirche in Deutschland, 1992.
Raming, Ida. "'Die zwölf Apostel waren Männer...'. Stereotype Einwände gegen die Frauenordination und ihre tieferen Ursachen." Orientierung 56 (1992): 143–46.

1993

"Frauenordination (volume theme)." Theologische Quartalschrift 173 (1993): 161–264.
Jensen, Anne. "Christusrepräsentation, kirchliche Ämter und Vorsitz bei der Eucharistie. Zur heutigen relecture einer frühchristlichen Tradition." Freiburger Zeitschrift für Philosophie und Theologie 40 (1993): 282–297.
Müller, Iris. "Priesteramt – für Männer eine Ehre – für Frauen ein Tabu." 37–43 in: Keine Frau schweige in der Kirche!, edited by Initiative Gleichberechtigung für Frauen in der Kirche, 1993.
Ohme, Heinz. "Die orthodoxe Kirche und die Ordination von Frauen. Zur Konferenz von Rhodus vom 30. Oktober bis 7. November 1988." Ökumenische Rundschau 42 (1993): 52–65.
Scheißl, Johanna. "Priestertum der Frau." Stimmen der Zeit 211 (1993): 115–122.

1994

"Apostolisches Schreiben, von Papst Johannes Paul II. Über die nur Männern vorbehaltene Priesterweihe (Ordinatio Sacerdotalis) vom 22.5.1994."3–7. Bonn, 1994.
"Das Apostolische Schreiben Ordinatio Sacerdotalis, vom 22.5.1994. Wortlaut – Stellungnahmen – Reaktionen." Klerusblatt 74 (1994): 147–151.
"Gott ist in Christus Mensch, nicht Mann geworden. Zur Ablehnung der Frauenordination in dem vatikanischen Schreiben über die Priesterweihe." Ökumenische Rundschau 43 (1994): 332f.
"Keine Priesterweihe von Frauen. Das Apostolische Schreiben Ordinatio Sacerdotalis mit den Erläuterungen im 'Osservatore Romano'." Herder Korrespondenz 48 (1994): 356–358.

Antón, Angel. "'Ordinatio Sacerdotalis.' Algunas reflexiones de 'gnoseiología teológica'." Gregorianum 75 (1994): 723–742.

Beinert, Wolfgang. "Priestertum der Frau. Der Vorhang zu, die Frage offen?" Stimmen der Zeit, 212 (1994): 723–738.

Brunelli, Lucio and Andrea Tornielli. "Frauen als Priester. Der Fall ist abgeschlossen." 30 Tage 30:6 (1994): 10–13.

Geldbach, Erich. "Endgültiges Nein Roms zur Priesterweihe von Frauen." Materialdienst des Konfessionskundlichen Instituts Bensheim 45 (1994): 65–67.

Hälbig, Klaus W. "'Er hat sie durch sein Blut gereinigt'. Zur Frage der Frauenordination im Horizont sakramentalen Denkens." Internationale Katholische Zeitschrift Communio 23 (1994): 345–359.

Hünermann, Peter. "Schwerwiegende Bedenken. Eine Analyse des Apostolischen Schreibens Ordinatio Sacerdotalis." Herder Korrespondenz 48 (1994): 406–410.

Jensen, Anne. "Ist Frauenordination ein ökumenisches Problem? Zu den jüngsten Entwicklungen in den anglikanischen, altkatholischen und orthodoxen Kirchen." Internationale kirchliche Zeitschrift 84 (1994): 210–228.

Nientiedt, Klaus. "Bischofskonferenz: Spannungen nehmen zu." Herder Korrespondenz 48 (1994): 549–551.

Raming, Ida. "Endgültiges Nein zum Priestertum der Frau? Zum Apostolischen Schreiben Johannes Pauls II Ordinatio Sacerdotalis." Orientierung 58 (1994): 190–193.

"Ungenutzte Chancen für Frauen im Kirchenrecht. Widersprüche im CIC/1983 und ihre Konsequenzen." Orientierung 58 (1994):68–70.

Ratzinger, Joseph. "Grenzen kirchlicher Vollmacht. Das neue Dokument von Papst Johannes Paul II. Zur Frage der Frauenordination." Internationale Katholische Zeitschrift 23 (1994): 337–345.

Ruh, Ulrich. "Die Würfel sind gefallen. In der Kirche von England empfingen erstmals Frauen die Priesterweihe." Herder Korrespondenz 48 (1994): 176–180.

"Lehramt im Abseits?" Herder Korrespondenz 48 (1994): 325–327.

Seibel, Wolfgang. "Priestertum der Frau." Stimmen der Zeit 212 (1994): 577f.

1995

Hauke, Manfred. 'Ordinatio Sacerdotalis'. Das päpstliche Schreiben zum Frauenpriestertum im Spiegel der Diskussion." Forum Katholische Theologie 11 (1995): 270–298.

Küng, Hans. "Das Nein zur Frauenordination – unfehlbar! Anti-Priesterinnen-Dekret des Vatikans stellt Theologen vor Entscheidung. Süddeutsche Zeitung 2:12 (1995): 10.

Laurien, Hanna-Renate. Abgeschrieben? Plädoyer für eine faire Diskussion über das Priestertum der Frau. Freiburg: Herder, 1995.

Raming, Ida. "Priesteramt für Frauen: Eine Forderung der Gerechtigkeit und Anerkennung ihres Christseins." Katechetische Blätter 120 (1995): 296–299.

1996

Gössman, Elisabeth. "Die 'Braut Kirche' und der Priester als 'Bräutigam' Rom und das neue Exempel männlicher Macht. Zum Verbot der Priesterweihe von Frauen." Frankfurter Rundschau 5:2 (1996): 12.

Groß, Walter, ed. Frauenordination. Stand der Diskussion in der katholischen Kirche. München: E. Wewel Verlag, 1996.

Hafner, Felix and Denis Buser. Frauenordination via Gleichstellungsgesetz? Die Anwendbarkeit des Gleichstellungsgesetzes auf die Dienstverhältnisse in der römisch-katholischen Kirche. Aktuelle Juristische Praxis (1996): 1207–1214.

Hausten, Jörg. "Unfehlbar, aber nicht unwiderrufbar? Zum Diskurs um die Ablehnung der Frauenordination." Materialdienst des Konfessionskundlichen Instituts Bensheim (1996): 21f.

Lüdecke, Norbert. "Also doch ein Dogma? Fragen zum Verbindllichkeitsanspruch der Lehre über die Unmöglichkeit der Priesterweihe für Frauen aus kanonistische Perspektive." Trierer Theologische Zeitschrift 105 (1996): 161–121.

Nientiedt, Klaus. "Eine weitere Etappe. Zur Priesterweihe von Frauen bei den deutschen Altkatholiken." Herder Korrespondenz 50 (1996): 352–355.

Raberger, Walter. "'Ordinationsfähigkeit' der Frau? Anmerkungen zum Thema 'Frauenpriestertum'." Theologisch-praktische Quartalschrift 144 (1996): 398–411.

Raming, Ida. "Für die Rechte der Frauen in der Kirche. Eindrücke und Überlegungen zur Women's Ordination Conference 1995." Orientierung 60 (1996): 54–57.

Ruprecht, Sabine. "Frauenordination in der Kirche von England. Ein Bericht."
Pastoraltheologie 85 (1996): 190–195.

Vobbe, Joachim, ed. "'Geh zu meinen Brüdern'. Vom priesterlichen Auftrag und Amt der Frauen in der Kirche. Brief des Bischofs an die Gemeinden des Katholischen Bistums der Alt-Katholiken. Bonn: Kath. Bistum der Alt-Katholiken in Deutschland, 1996.

1997

"Frauenordination und Tradition. Stellungnahme der 'Catholic Theological Society of America'. "Herder Korrespondenz 51 (1997): 414–419.

Professorenkollegium der Bonner Katholisch-Theologischen Fakultät, ed. Projekttag Frauenordination. Alfter: Borengässer, 1997.

Rigl, Thomas. "Kontext und Begründung der Frauenordination in der Kirche von England." Catholica 51 (1997): 3–31.

Schwarz, Roland. "Verbieten Bibeltexte die Frauenordination?" Diakonia 28 (1997): 167–173.

1998

Müller, Iris and Ida Raming. Aufbruch aus männlichen "Gottesordnungen". Reformbestrebungen von Frauen in christlichen Kirchen und im Islam. Weinheim: Dt. Studien Verlag, 1998.

Raming, Ida, Gertrud Jansen et. al., eds. Zur Priesterin berufen. Gott sieht nicht auf das Geschlecht. Zeugnisse römisch-katholischer Frauen. München, Schnell & Steiner, 1998.

1999

Buser, Denise and Adrian Loretan, eds. Gleichstellung der Geschlechter und die Kirchen. Ein Beitrag zur menschenrechtlichen und ökumenischen Diskussion. Freiburg: Universitätsverlag Freiburg Schweiz, 1999.

Müller, Gerhard L., ed. Der Empfänger des Weihesakraments. Quellen zur Lehre und Praxis der Kirche, nur Männern das Weihesakrament zu spenden. Würzberg: Echter, 1999.

2000

Bock, Wolfgang and Wolfgang Lienemann, eds. Frauenordination. Studien zu Kirchenrecht und Theologie, 3 vols. Heidelberg: FEST, 2000.

Macy, Gary. "The Ordination of Women in the Early Middle Ages." Theological Studies 61 (2000): 481–507.

Müller, Gerhard L. Priestertum und Diakonat. Der Empfänger des Weihesakramentes in schöpfungstheologischer und christologischer Perspektive. Freiburg: Herder, 2000.

Raming, Ida. "Frauen suchen Antworten. Reaktionen auf frauenfeindliche Blockaden." Orientierung 64 (2000): 100–103, 111–114.

2001

Raming, Ida. "Frauen gegen Diskriminierung und Entrechtung. Entstehung und Entwicklung der Frauenordinationsbewegung in der katholischen Kirche Europas." Orientierung 65 (2001): 75–79, 86–91.

2002

Ertel, Werner/Forster, Gisela (Hg.): "Wir sind Priesterinnen". Aus aktuellem Anlass: Die Weihe von Frauen 2002, Düsseldorf: Patmos-Verlag 2002.

Raming, Ida: Priesteramt der Frau – Geschenk Gottes für eine erneuerte Kirche (erweiterte Neuauflage von "Der Ausschluss der Frau vom priesterlichen Amt", 1973) LIT-Verlag 2002

2003

Liebelt, Markus: Frauenordination: Ein Beitrag zur gegenwärtigen Diskussion im evangelikalen Kontext, Nürnberg, Ed. Bibelbund, 2003

2004

Demel, Sabine: Frauen und kirchliches Amt. Vom Ende eines Tabus in der katholischen Kirche, Freiburg Herder-Verlag 2004.

Ansorge, Nadine: Gisbert Greshake und das Thema 'Ordination der Frau'. München: GRIN 2004.

Sepp, Peter: Geheime Weihen: die Frauen in der verborgenen tschechoslovakischen Kirche Koinótes, Ostfildern: Schwabenverlag 2004.

2006

Egger, Monika (Hg.): Woman in Church: Kirche und Amt im Kontext der Geschlechterfrage, Berlin LIT-Verlag 2006.

Gröne, Stephan: Kontra Frauenordination: Warum Jesus die Gemeindeleitung durch Frauen verbietet, Verlag: Hamburg: Mein Buch.

Ahlers, Stella: Gleichstellung der Frau in Staat und Kirche – ein problematisches Spannungsverhältnis. Berlin: LIT Verlag 2006

Raming, Ida: Gleichrangig in Christus anstatt: Ausschluss von Frauen 'im Namen Gottes'. Berlin: LIT Verlag 2006.

Müller, Gerhard Ludwig (Hg.): Von Inter Insigniores bis Ordinatio Sacerdotalis. Dokumente der Glaubenskongregation. Würzburg: Echter-Verlag 2006

2007

Gröne, Stephan: Frauenordination und Schöpfungsordnung: Warum Jesus die Gemeindeleitung durch Frauen verbietet. Verlag Fuchstal 2007.

Müller, Iris / Raming, Ida: Unser Leben im Einsatz für Menschenrechte der Frauen in der römisch-katholischen Kirche. Berlin LIT-Verlag 2007.

2008

Simon, Susanne: Jesus und die Frauen im Spiegel seiner Zeit und dessen Bedeutung für die Frauenordination, München: GRIN Verlag 2008.
Kress, Ursula (Hg.): Grüß Gott, Frau Pfarrerin! 40 Jahre Theologinnenordnung. Stuttgart: Kreuz-Verlag 2008.

2009

Hainz McGrath, Elsie u.a. (Hg.): Frauen finden einen Weg: Die internationale Bewegung Römisch-katholische Priesterinnen, Berlin: LIT Verlag 2009

2012

Kliver, Christian P.: Frauenordination versus Heilige Schrift? Kaufbeuren: Port-Royal Verlag 2012
Berger, Klaus: Priesterweihe auch für Frauen? Münster: Aschendorf Verlag 2012.

2013

Raming, Ida: Römisch-katholische Priesterinnen. Realität in der gegenwärtigen und zukünftigen Kirche. Berlin: LIT-Verlag 2013

2015

Beyer, Johanna (Hg.): 40 Jahre Frauenordination (Festschrift) München: Frauengleichstellungsstelle, Landeskirchenamt 2015.
Grave, Sr. Ingrid u.a. (Hg.): Frauen in der Kirche? Unverzichtbar. Freiburg/Schweiz Paulusverlag 2015.

2016

Jung, Friedhelm: Die Stellung der Frau nach Gottes Plan. Licht-Zeichen Verlag 2016.
Straub, Jaqueline: Jung, katholisch, weiblich. Weshalb ich Priesterin werden will. Oberursel: Publik-Forum Verlagsgesellschaft, 2016.
Weber, Quirin: Frauenordination – Notwendendes 'Zeichen der Zeit'. SKZ 37/2016.

2017

Buschan, Christian: Frauenordination versus Frauenfeindlichkeit in den christlichen Kirchen. Saarbrücken. Fromm Verlag 2017.

Zeiß-Horbach, Auguste: Evangelische Kirche und Frauenordination: der Beitrag der Evangelisch-Lutherischen Kirche in Bayern zur deutschlandweiten Diskussion im 20. Jahrhundert. Leipzig: Evangelische Verlagsanstalt 2017.

Lüdecke, Norbert: Also doch ein Dogma? Fragen zum Verbindlichkeitsanspruch der Lehre über die Unmöglichkeit der Priesterweihe für Frauen aus kanonistischer Perspektive. Bonn: Unversitäts- u. Landesbibliothek 2017.

Florin, Christiane: Der Weiberaufstand. Warum Frauen in der katholischen Kirche mehr Macht brauchen. München: Kösel-Verlag 2017.

Härle, Wilfried: Von Christus beauftragt. Ein biblisches Plädoyer für Ordination und Priesterweihe von Frauen. Ev. Verlagsanstalt Leipzig 2017.

Loretan, Adrian: Wahrheitsansprüche im Kontext der Freiheitsrechte. (Religionsrechtliche Studien 3) Zürich, Theologischer Verlag 2017.

2018

Airne, Pierre: Frauen auf der Kanzel. Frauenordination und FrauenPfarramt in den reformierten Kirchen der Schweiz. Theologischer Verlag Zürich 2018.

Theologie: Forschung und Wissenschaft

Leonardo Boff
Traum von einer neuen Erde – Bilanz eines theologischen Lebens
Deutsche Übersetzung: Bruno Kern
„‚Ich habe einen Traum ... ‘Diese Worte aus der berühmten Rede, die Martin Luther King (1929 – 1968) kurz vor seinem Tod gehalten hat, kommen mir nun in den Sinn, da ich über achtzig Jahre alt und seit mehr als fünfzig Jahren Theologe bin. Ich blicke nun auf meine Zeit als Theologe zurück, die ich in diesem kleinen Buch darstellen will, doch meine Gedanken sind bei den jungen Leuten und mein Geist ist der Ewigkeit zugewandt."
So beginnt Leonardo Boff selbst diese kleine Bilanz seines Lebens und Wirkens als Theologe. Seine Beiträge zur Systematischen Theologie, zur Trinitätslehre, zur Christologie, zur Pneumatologie und zur Ekklesiologie, waren teilweise heftig umstritten, aber immer höchst fruchtbar und anregend.
Boffs Verdienst ist es aber vor allem, die Befreiungstheologie konsequent zu einer Ökotheologie der Befreiung weiterentwickelt zu haben. Im Gespräch mit der neuen Kosmologie, der Quantenphysik, der Tiefenökologie, etc. entfaltet er hier ein neues Paradigma für die Theologie auf der Höhe der Zeit. Diese kleine Summe von Boffs theologischem Denken ist zugleich eine zutiefst spirituelle Lektüre.
Bd. 64, 2019, 212 S., 19,90 €, br., ISBN 978-3-643-91113-1

John Corrigan; Frank Hinkelmann (eds.)
Return to Sender
American Evangelical Missions to Europe in the 20th Century
This collection of studies by American and European scholars explores the various ways in which American evangelicals found their way to postwar Europe, what they did there, and how they were received. With attention to the American and European organizations that brokered their mission, the social and political settings that framed their activities, and the mixed results of their efforts, these studies provide a much-needed overview how an important twentieth-century style of Christianity "returned" to Europe.
Bd. 63, 2019, 152 S., 29,90 €, br., ISBN 978-3-643-91083-7

Josef Nolte
Savonarola – Michelangelo – Luther
Ergänzungen zur Reformationsgeschichte und weiterreichende Fragen
Bd. 61, 2018, 240 S., 34,90 €, br., ISBN 978-3-643-13857-6

Cloe Taddei-Ferretti
Even the Dogs
The Ordination of Women in the Catholic Church
A hystorical *excursus*: women ministries in early Church; disputed traces of women presbyteral ministry; women diaconal ministry, and differences in ordination rite and functions for deaconesses and deacons of Byzantine Church. The value of person and of reciprocity asks today for identical ordination rite and functions of deaconesses and deacons.
The analysis of hypothetical possibility of women presbyteral ordination: belief in women subordination; spousal symbol; Mary; woman and person; reciprocity; incarnation of the Word; impossibility of women presbyteral vocation; value of doctrines; sacramental sign and substance of a sacrament. A prayer for women presbyteral ordination is proposed.
Bd. 60, 2017, 276 S., 34,90 €, br., ISBN 978-3-643-90927-5

Michael Hoelzl
Theorie vom guten Hirten
Eine kurze Geschichte pastoralen Herrschaftswissens
Bd. 59, 2017, 324 S., 39,90 €, br., ISBN 978-3-643-90863-6

Tomislav Ivančić
Jesus aus Nazareth – geschichtliche Person
Zugänge im Blick auf fundamentale Rückfragen aus Theologie, Geschichts-, Literatur- und Kulturwissenschaft
Bd. 58, 2018, 184 S., 29,90 €, gb., ISBN 978-3-643-13617-6

LIT Verlag Berlin – Münster – Wien – Zürich – London
Auslieferung Deutschland / Österreich / Schweiz: siehe Impressumsseite

Ida Raming
55 Jahre Kampf für Frauenordination in der katholischen Kirche
Eine Pionierin hält Rückschau: Personen – Dokumente – Ereignisse – Bewegungen
55 Jahre Kampf für Frauenordination in der römisch-katholischen Kirche — dieser lebenslange Einsatz der Theologin Ida Raming – gemeinsam mit gleichgesinnten, teils schon verstorbenen Pionierinnen – wird in der vorliegenden Dokumentation dargestellt.
Beginnend mit dem Vatikanischen Konzil (1962 – 1965) zieht sich dieser Einsatz durch mehrere kirchengeschichtliche Phasen hindurch bis hin zur Gegenwart. Aus der Perspektive der Autorin werden anhand zahlreicher Dokumente innerkirchliche Entwicklungen, Konflikte und internationale Bewegungen bis hin zur Gegenwart lebendig und anschaulich vor Augen geführt.
Für das Studium dieser wichtigen kirchengeschichtlichen Epoche seit 1962 bis heute ist diese Dokumentation ein ausgezeichnetes Hilfsmittel.
Bd. 62, 2018, 138 S., 19,90 €, br., ISBN 978-3-643-14031-9

Theologische Plädoyers

Ida Raming
Römisch-katholische Priesterinnen
Realität in der gegenwärtigen und zukünftigen Kirche!
Bd. 6, 2013, 136 S., 16,90 €, br., ISBN 978-3-643-12307-7

Ida Raming
Gleichrangig in Christus anstatt: Ausschluss von Frauen „im Namen Gottes"
Zur Rezeption und Interpretation von Gal 3,27f in vatikanischen Dokumenten
Bd. 1, 2006, 120 S., 10,00 €, br., ISBN 3-8258-9706-0

Theologische Orientierungen
Theological Orientations

Ida Raming; Iris Müller
"Contra Legem" – a Matter of Conscience
Our Lifelong Struggle for Human Rights for Women in the Roman-Catholic Church. Autobiographies, Background Papers, Documents, Future Prospects
Bd. 15, 2011, 296 S., 24,90 €, br., ISBN 3-643-10986-6

Iris Müller; Ida Raming
Unser Leben im Einsatz für Menschenrechte der Frauen in der römisch-katholischen Kirche
Lebensberichte – Hintergründe – Dokumente – Ausblick
Bd. 4, 2007, 264 S., 17,90 €, br., ISBN 978-3-8258-0186-1

★★★

Dietrich Bäuerle
Kirche – Frauen – Menschenrechte
Impulse aus dem Leben der Maria Magdalena für eine andere Kirche
KirchenZukunft konkret, Bd. 14, 2019, 144 S., 19,90 €, br., ISBN 978-3-643-14425-6

Helen Schüngel-Straumann
Feministische Theologie und Gender
Interdisziplinäre Perspektiven
Internationale Forschungen in Feministischer Theologie und Religion. Befreiende Perspektiven, Bd. 4, 2015, 240 S., 29,90 €, br., ISBN-CH 978-3-643-80191-3

Elisabeth Schüssler Fiorenza
Grenzen überschreiten: Der theoretische Anspruch feministischer Theologie
Ausgewählte Aufsätze
Theologische Frauenforschung in Europa, Bd. 15, 2. Aufl. 2007, 264 S., 24,90 €, br., ISBN 978-3-8258-7166-5

Irmtraud Fischer; Christoph Heil (Hg.)
Geschlechterverhältnisse und Macht
Lebensformen in der Zeit des frühen Christentums
Exegese in unserer Zeit. Kontextuelle Bibelinterpretationen, Bd. 21, 2010, 312 S., 29,90 €, br., ISBN-AT 978-3-643-50218-6

Daniela Müller
Frauen und Häresie
Europas christliches Erbe
Christentum und Dissidenz, Bd. 2, 2015, 216 S., 34,90 €, gb., ISBN 978-3-643-12743-3

LIT Verlag Berlin – Münster – Wien – Zürich – London
Auslieferung Deutschland / Österreich / Schweiz: siehe Impressumsseite

Melanie Kolm
Frauen in der Katholischen Kirche – betroffen und beteiligt
Ekklesiologische Reflexionen über nachkonziliare synodale Prozesse
Theologische Frauenforschung in Europa, Bd. 27, 2016, 590 S., 59,90 €, br., ISBN 978-3-643-12632-0

Lydia Bendel-Maidl (Hg.)
Katholikinnen im 20. Jahrhundert
Bilder, Rollen, Aufgaben
Beiträge zu Theologie, Kirche und Gesellschaft im 20. Jahrhundert, Bd. 2, 2007, 328 S., 24,90 €, br., ISBN 978-3-8258-5540-6

Wolfgang Vogl; Sebastian Walser (Hg.)
Geistliche Frauen des 20. Jahrhunderts
Wieder- und Neuentdeckungen
Theologie des geistlichen Lebens, Bd. 1, 2019, ca. 264 S., ca. 34,90 €, br., ISBN 978-3-643-13949-8

Stella Ahlers
Gleichstellung der Frau in Staat und Kirche – ein problematisches Spannungsverhältnis
ReligionsRecht im Dialog / Law and Religion, Bd. 2, 2005, 256 S., 19,90 €, br., ISBN-DE 3-8258-8751-0, ISBN-CH 3-03735-216-7

Julia Bruch
Die Zisterze Kaisheim und ihre Tochterklöster
Studien zur Organisation und zum Wirtschaften spätmittelalterlicher Frauenklöster mit einer Edition des „Kaisheimer Rechnungsbuches"
Vita regularis – Editionen, Bd. 5, 2013, 688 S., 69,90 €, br., ISBN 978-3-643-12370-1

Virginia Azcuy; Margit Eckholt (Hg.)
Citizenship – Biographien – Institutionen
Perspektiven lateinamerikanischer und deutscher Theologinnen auf Kirche und Gesellschaft
Bd. 1, 2009, 272 S., 19,90 €, br., ISBN 978-3-8258-1198-3

Monika Egger; Livia Meier; Katja Wißmiller (Hg.)
WoMan in Church
Kirche und Amt im Kontext der Geschlechterfrage
Theologische Frauenforschung in Europa, Bd. 20, 2006, 152 S., 19,90 €, br., ISBN-DE 3-8258-9220-4, ISBN-CH 3-03735-104-7

Susanne Gäßler
Die Entdeckung der menschlichen Würde
Jüdische Lebenswelt und humanistische Lebensgestaltung bei Friedrich Georg Friedmann
Forum Christen und Juden, Bd. 2, 2002, 216 S., 19,90 €, br., ISBN 3-8258-6326-3

Maria Elisabeth Aigner; Ursula Rapp (Hg.)
KlarA. Klar anders!
Mentoring für Wissenschafterinnen
Werkstatt Theologie – Praxisorientierte Studien und Diskurse, Bd. 19, 2011, 144 S., 19,90 €, br., ISBN-AT 978-3-643-50294-0

Jobst Reller (Hg.)
„Die Mission ist weiblich"
Frauen in der frühen Hermannsburger Mission
Quellen und Beiträge zur Geschichte der Hermannsburger Mission und des Ev.-luth. Missionswerkes in Niedersachsen, Bd. 21, 2012, 216 S., 19,90 €, br., ISBN 978-3-643-11547-8

LIT Verlag Berlin – Münster – Wien – Zürich – London
Auslieferung Deutschland / Österreich / Schweiz: siehe Impressumsseite